MICAH

MICAH

Proclaiming the Incomparable God

Martyn McGeown

REFORMED
FREE PUBLISHING
ASSOCIATION
Jenison, Michigan

Scripture cited is taken from the King James (Authorized) Version

Reformed Free Publishing Association
1894 Georgetown Center Drive
Jenison, Michigan 49428
616-457-5970
www.rfpa.org
mail@rfpa.org

Cover design by Erika Kiel
Interior design and typeset by Katherine Lloyd/theDESKonline.com

ISBN: 978-1-944555-41-2 (hardcover)
ISBN: 978-1-944555-42-9 (ebook)
LCCN: 2018947925

"And beginning at Moses and all the prophets, he expounded unto them in all the scriptures the things concerning himself."

Luke 24:27

CONTENTS

PREFACE

For many years the minor prophets have fascinated me. If you have read multiple times through the Bible as I have, you might have been bewildered at these twelve short, but difficult books at the end of the Old Testament. Perhaps as a child you memorized the list of the books of the Bible—including Hosea through Malachi—but even now you feel embarrassed when the minister announces Habakkuk, Haggai, Obadiah, or Micah from the pulpit because you cannot find them without checking the contents page of your Bible.

And even if you do find Micah or one of the other short prophetic books, you do not know what any of it (with the possible exception of Jonah) means. Yes, you are familiar with a few passages from the prophets, but these books remain largely a mystery. With a sigh, resigned that you will never grasp the meaning, you dutifully read through the prophets until finally you reach the easier New Testament.

But the minor prophets are part of scripture. They are inspired writings addressed to the people of God, and addressed to us also in the New Testament church. As inspired scripture they speak of Christ: Micah speaks of Christ and not only in the obvious reference to Bethlehem in chapter 5:2. Christians want to know Christ also from the Old Testament, from Micah, and the other minor prophets. And yet for many of us the minor prophets are like a sealed book.

This book is based on a series of sermons that I preached in Limerick, Ireland, between November 2013 and March 2014, to the saints of the Limerick Reformed Fellowship. I present it with the prayer that the reader might find in the prophecy of Micah the incomparable God of glory in our Lord Jesus Christ.

INTRODUCTION

One of the most neglected portions of scripture is the minor prophets. We neglect them because they are difficult to understand and seemingly distant from us. Micah the prophet is distant from us historically, geographically, and culturally, but Micah's prophecy is part of holy scripture, and he speaks to us today. Micah is one of the twelve minor prophets (Hosea to Malachi); minor not because he is unimportant, but because of his relative brevity.

Micah is best known for three passages:

> But thou, Bethlehem Ephratah, though thou be little among the thousands of Judah, yet out of thee shall he come forth unto me that is to be ruler in Israel; whose goings forth have been from of old, from everlasting. (5:2)

> He hath shewed thee, O man, what is good; and what doth the Lord require of thee, but to do justly, and to love mercy, and to walk humbly with thy God? (6:8)

> Who is a God like unto thee, that pardoneth iniquity, and passeth by the transgression of the remnant of his heritage? he retaineth not his anger for ever, because he delighteth in mercy. (7:18)

Micah's name means "Who is like Jehovah?" and his message is to proclaim the incomparable God. No god is like Jehovah in judgment, righteousness, and holiness. No god is like Jehovah in mercy and faithfulness.

We need to place Micah in the broad sweep of biblical history. Micah prophesied some two hundred years after the division of the kingdom of Israel and some one hundred and fifty years before the Babylonian captivity. Micah was a prophet during the reigns of Jotham, Ahaz, and Hezekiah (1:1). This makes Micah a contemporary of Isaiah (who began prophesying before Micah) and Hosea (who prophesied around the same time as Micah).

Furthermore, Micah prophesied near the end of the northern kingdom of Israel, shortly before Samaria fell to the Assyrians in 722 BC. Micah prophesied to Judah while she had one of the worst and then one of the best kings of her history. Jotham was good, Ahaz was very wicked, and Hezekiah was the great reformatory king. Yet even during Hezekiah's reign, the people as a whole were living in hypocrisy. The people of Judah imagined that God could never judge them because they were God's people, for God dwelt in their midst. Therefore, they lived in presumption. The great world power of that day was Assyria, which would destroy the northern kingdom near the beginning of Hezekiah's reign and even attempt to overthrow Judah. God gave Judah a reprieve of some one hundred and fifty years before judgment fell on Jerusalem. Interestingly, Micah's message brought Hezekiah's generation to repentance:

17. Then rose up certain of the elders of the land, and spake to all the assembly of the people, saying,

18. Micah the Morasthite prophesied in the days of Hezekiah king of Judah, and spake to all the people of Judah, saying, Thus saith the Lord of hosts; Zion shall be plowed like a field, and Jerusalem shall become

heaps, and the mountain of the house as the high places of a forest.

19. Did Hezekiah king of Judah and all Judah put him at all to death? did he not fear the Lord, and besought the Lord, and the Lord repented him of the evil which he had pronounced against them? Thus might we procure great evil against our souls. (Jer. 26:17–19)

About Micah himself we possess very few details: he is simply called the Morasthite (Mic. 1:1), which means that he was a native of the Judean town of Moresheth-gath (v. 14). His prophecy can be neatly divided into three sections beginning with the command to hear: chapters 1–2 ("Hear, all ye people"), chapters 3–5 ("And I said, Hear, I pray you"), and chapters 6–7 ("Hear ye now what the Lord saith").

Before we begin, we need to see some general truths about prophecy. First, prophets do not merely or even mainly predict the future. A prophet was a messenger of God to whom the word of God came. The word *prophet* in Hebrew comes from a verb that means "to bubble forth."

Second, prophets receive direct revelation from God. God speaks to them, they see visions, and they dream dreams. Therefore, what they proclaim is the authoritative word of God ("The word of the Lord that came to Micah…which he saw" [1:1]).

Third, the prophets couch their prophecy in figurative language, using language familiar to their audience, the language of the Old Testament. Thus they speak of cities known to the people, religious ordinances practiced by the people, and other aspects of Old Testament life unfamiliar to us.

Fourth, the prophets use a device called "foreshortening," which means that they see multiple events as one single event. The first and second comings of Christ are one event from their vantage point. Rarely, if ever, do they provide specific times or dates: "the last times," "the latter days," or "the last days" are as precise as they get.

Fifth, prophets prophesy to God's people and for the sake of the elect. The prophets do not offer answers to social issues. They address moral issues in the church, that is, the Old Testament church.

Sixth, the prophets address the nation as one organic whole. They bring a message of judgment to the whole nation in order to bring the elect to repentance. They proclaim salvation to the whole nation so that the elect will be comforted. When judgment falls, it falls on the whole nation: it destroys the reprobate and purifies the elect. The principle of Romans 9:6 must always be applied: "Not as though the word of God hath taken none effect. For they are not all Israel, which are of Israel."

Seventh, the prophets speak of Christ. They speak of him in Old Testament picture language suitable to their times, but they do speak of him. We must see Christ in the prophets:

> And beginning at Moses and all the prophets, he expounded unto them in all the scriptures the things concerning himself. (Luke 24:27)

10. Of which salvation the prophets have inquired and searched diligently, who prophesied of the grace that should come unto you:

11. Searching what, or what manner of time the Spirit of Christ which was in them did signify, when it testified beforehand the sufferings of Christ, and the glory that should follow.

12. Unto whom it was revealed, that not unto themselves, but unto us they did minister the things, which are now reported unto you by them that have preached the gospel unto you with the Holy Ghost sent down

from heaven; which things the angels desire to look into. (1 Pet. 1:10–12)

With these principles guiding the reader, we begin our study of the prophecy of Micah as he reveals to us the word of the incomparable God.

Chapter 1

Mountain-Melting Judgment

1. The word of the Lord that came to Micah the Moras-thite in the days of Jotham, Ahaz, and Hezekiah, kings of Judah, which he saw concerning Samaria and Jerusalem.
2. Hear, all ye people; hearken, O earth, and all that therein is: and let the Lord God be witness against you, the Lord from his holy temple.
3. For, behold, the Lord cometh forth out of his place, and will come down, and tread upon the high places of the earth.
4. And the mountains shall be molten under him, and the valleys shall be cleft, as wax before the fire, and as the waters that are poured down a steep place.
5. For the transgression of Jacob is all this, and for the sins of the house of Israel. What is the transgression of Jacob? is it not Samaria? and what are the high places of Judah? are they not Jerusalem?
6. Therefore I will make Samaria as an heap of the field, and as plantings of a vineyard: and I will pour down the stones thereof into the valley, and I will discover the foundations thereof.

7. And all the graven images thereof shall be beaten to pieces, and all the hires thereof shall be burned with the fire, and all the idols thereof will I lay desolate: for she gathered it of the hire of an harlot, and they shall return to the hire of an harlot. (Micah 1:1–7)

THE MEANING

Micah begins with judgment: a terrifying, awe-inspiring description of God as judge. In this first vision, Micah presents Jehovah as both judge and witness. From this we are immediately struck by two truths.

First, Jehovah is not a local deity, a national god, but the God of all the earth. Sometimes Israel was tempted to think that Jehovah lived in the temple in Jerusalem as if he were confined there, but such a thought domesticated God, manipulated him, and dishonored him. Micah begins (literally) in verse 2: "Hear ye *peoples*, all of them; hearken, earth and its fullness" (emphasis added). In chapter 6, Micah includes the mountains and hills (vv. 1–2). God claims sovereign jurisdiction over all peoples, not only over Israel and Judah. This is because Jehovah is the creator and lord of all: "The earth is the LORD's, and the fulness thereof; the world, and they that dwell therein" (Ps. 24:1).

Second, Jehovah summons all men to witness and participate in court proceedings or in a trial. This is a summons that no man can put off or ignore. The language of our text is that of the courtroom. Hear and hearken! Pay attention while the judge presides! Be silent before him, for he has something to say! Jehovah is not only the judge, but also the witness, the witness for the prosecution. A witness gives testimony in a court of what he has seen, heard, and known. Jehovah has seen, heard, and known all things. That he is the prosecuting witness and not the defense witness is seen in the word *against*: "Let the Lord GOD be witness *against* you" (Mic. 1:2, emphasis added).

On the basis of God's own testimony, he will pronounce judgment and condemn. He will pronounce sentence and punish. Who else would dare make this claim? None of the heathen gods claimed such universal power and authority. None of the heathen gods claimed to judge all peoples.

The sting for Micah's hearers, probably gathered around him in Jerusalem, is that God's judgment includes and even begins with his own people, Israel and Judah. Micah did not go to all the nations of the earth (Assyria, Egypt, Philistia, and so on) and tell them this word of God. He proclaimed this to Israel and Judah. Probably as Micah begins to speak, the people are pleased with the message. "God is a witness against all peoples. Good. God will judge all peoples. Excellent. That is what we want." But that is not where Micah ends. Micah very quickly turns from all peoples (v. 2) to God's own people (v. 5). Micah changes from general judgment to specific judgment.

Micah's message is judgment against the church— the church of his day, and the church of all ages, which is guilty of the same sins described in this book. There is a very important principle here. Judgment begins with the house of God (1 Pet. 4:17). Before God destroys the wicked, he will purge his church through judgment, purify her, bring her to repentance, and destroy the wicked within her. That is the offense of the prophet; that made him offensive to Israel some 2,700 years ago, and that makes him offensive to us today. When we study Micah, we must not say, "Oh, how wicked those Jews were!" We must rather confess, "How wicked I am!" We must not lose sight of our own sins.

That is not popular preaching. The church will tolerate sermons about sin as long as they are sermons about the sins of the world, sermons about the sins of the false church, or sermons about the sins of the neighbor. But Israel and Judah did not want Micah to preach about her sins, and we do not welcome the preacher preaching about our sins today: "But truly I am full of power by the spirit of the LORD, and of judgment, and of might, to declare unto Jacob his transgression, and to Israel his sin" (Mic. 3:8).

Very graphically and vividly, Micah describes the judgment of Jehovah upon Israel. He does so in terms of Jehovah descending, or coming down, and treading or trampling upon the mountains. The description of Jehovah's descent is terrifying; it should be, especially to the wicked. As long as Jehovah remains in his holy temple, in his place, he appears distant, but in Micah's vision, Jehovah "cometh forth out of his place" (1:3). Jehovah comes forth because he has been provoked to wrath. He comes on a mission of destruction.

What is striking is that Jehovah "will come down" (v. 3). For Jehovah, you see, the only way is down. Everything is beneath him because he is the exalted creator and ruler over all things:

4. The Lord is high above all nations, and his glory above the heavens.
5. Who is like unto the Lord our God, who dwelleth on high,
6. Who humbleth himself to behold the things that are in heaven, and in the earth! (Ps. 113:4–6)

Jehovah, warns Micah, shall come down and tread upon the high places of the earth. The highest mountains are for this God, this incomparable God, low.

That is awesome, and we should ponder it. When we look at the mountains, we are awestruck at their height. Usually we cannot even see the top of them. Some very courageous human beings have attempted to climb such mountains, yet few have climbed the world's tallest peaks. But the world's tallest peak is nothing to Jehovah. He treads it underfoot. Is that your God? The God whose footstool is the mountains? The God who comes down to stand upon the highest mountain ranges? If not, he is too small.

God's judgment would fall first upon Samaria. "I will make Samaria as an heap of the field" (Mic. 1:6). That is the purpose of Jehovah's descent upon the mountains. Jehovah comes to judge and to destroy.

Samaria was the capital city of the northern kingdom of Israel, which Omri, Ahab's father, had built.

> 23. In the thirty and first year of Asa king of Judah began Omri to reign over Israel, twelve years: six years reigned he in Tirzah.
> 24. And he bought the hill Samaria of Shemer for two talents of silver, and built on the hill, and called the name of the city which he built, after the name of Shemer, owner of the hill, Samaria.
> 25. But Omri wrought evil in the eyes of the Lord, and did worse than all that were before him. (1 Kings 16:23–25)

Samaria was a heavily fortified city that stood on a hill. It had excellent protection, and the Israelites imagined it could never fall. They also imagined that it would never fall because God would protect it. But Israel had apostatized from the worship of Jehovah many years before Micah preached. Despite constant warnings from God's prophets, she never repented, and she never expected judgment to come. But judgment did come in 722 BC, when after a lengthy siege the Assyrians captured Samaria and with it the northern kingdom.

Samaria's destruction was utter and final. Worse, her destruction was of God.

Samaria was demolished so that she was "an heap" (Mic. 1:6), a ruin, fit only for planting vineyards on her fertile slopes. Even her foundations were uprooted and the stones of her buildings were dumped into the valley below. The people of Samaria and of Israel were slaughtered, and the survivors were rounded up as prisoners and scattered throughout the Assyrian empire. They never returned.

But notice verse 6: "I will make." God did this. He used Assyria as an instrument in his hand, but he did it. He came forth in power and wrath out of his place to do it. That is what was happening behind the scenes. Micah, with prophetic insight by divine revelation, saw that.

Do not miss that. And that is still true today: when a nation falls, whether by war, political intrigue, societal decadence, or some other factor, God brings that nation down. One day he will bring all nations down when he finally comes out of his holy place.

THE EFFECT

Jehovah's coming down in judgment has an effect upon the mountains: they melt. There is nothing more solid, more permanent in all creation than mountains. Mountains have been here a lot longer than we have; they have seen countless generations, and they will be here long after we have died. In scripture, mountains are a symbol of ancient stability. Only God himself is older than mountains, because he is eternal. "Before the mountains were settled, before the hills was I brought forth" (Prov. 8:25). "Before the mountains were brought forth...from everlasting to everlasting, thou art God" (Ps. 90:2).

The mountains round about Zion, which were by no means the highest mountains in the world, afforded protection to the city of Jerusalem and were symbolic of God's care for his church. "As the mountains are round about Jerusalem, so the LORD is round about his people from henceforth even for ever" (125:2). Can you imagine, then, that the mountains of Zion or the mountains of the Alps, Rockies, Andes, or Himalayas could ever be moved?

When Jehovah comes out of his place in judgment, the mountains not only move; they melt. That imagery is supposed to impress us. What kind of God causes the mountains to melt before him? Only the incomparable Jehovah! This melting of the mountains is not merely a volcanic eruption like the eruption of Mount Vesuvius or Mount Etna. This is the disintegration of the mountains themselves.

When Jehovah appears in judgment, the creation itself reacts.

The valleys are cleft, that is, they are split open or violently torn apart. Into the gaping abyss made by the cleft valleys flows the molten rock, which rushes down the slope like a torrent, an overwhelming flood. The mountains are like wax, which simply melts and is consumed when it comes into contact with fire. This kind of language appears in other passages as well.

5. The mountains quake at him, and the hills melt, and the earth is burned at his presence, yea, the world, and all that dwell therein.

6. Who can stand before his indignation? and who can abide in the fierceness of his anger? his fury is poured out like fire, and the rocks are thrown down by him...

8. But with an overrunning flood he will make an utter end of the place thereof, and darkness shall pursue his enemies. (Nah. 1:5–6, 8)

15. The kings...hid themselves in the dens and in the rocks of the mountains;

16. And said to the mountains and rocks, Fall on us, and hide us from the face of him that sitteth on the throne, and from the wrath of the Lamb. (Rev. 6:15–16)

This is a powerful, terrifying vision of the power and wrath of God. When Israel saw the marauding Assyrian armies, Micah saw Jehovah behind the army. This kind of language is common when describing earth-shattering judgments. When Samaria falls, when Judah falls, when Nineveh falls, when Babylon falls, Jehovah is coming forth out of his place to tread upon the high places of the earth. Micah was sent to proclaim this to God's people to stir them up to repentance.

This will really happen when Jesus Christ returns. Micah, like all prophets, sees something that has a near and far fulfillment. The ultimate fulfillment of this is the final judgment on the last day.

THE REASON

The reason for Jehovah's descending out of his holy place, the reason for the mountains melting, and the reason for Samaria becoming a heap is Israel's sin.

That was not what Israel and Judah were expecting to hear from the prophet. Remember, Micah 1:2 summons all peoples (plural) to be judged. Israel and Judah may have been expecting Micah to say: this judgment is coming because of Assyria's cruelty (Assyria was notorious for her barbarism), or this judgment is coming because of Egypt's idolatry. Verse 5 gives a different reason: "For the transgression of Jacob is all this, and for the sins of the house of Israel."

Israel's transgression was her rebellion against God. Israel, the northern kingdom, had rebelled against God for two centuries. That rebellion began at the start of the reign of Rehoboam when ten tribes seceded from Judah. At that point, the ten tribes cut themselves off from Jerusalem, the worship of God, the kings of David, and the line of Christ. Jeroboam I had made golden calves in Dan and Bethel, and later Israelite kings had continued to lead the people into idolatry.

In our text Israel's sin is especially called "the hire of an harlot" (v. 7). It ought to strike us that the prophets did not mince Jehovah's words. They used highly offensive language. A harlot, a whore or a prostitute, is one who sells her body to give sexual favors for money. The hire of a harlot is the price a man pays for the services of a harlot; it is the harlot's profit, how she makes a living. Micah accuses Israel of being a harlot and of gathering to herself idols and images with the hire of her harlotry. Israel's idols, in which she trusted, will be destroyed, she will be stripped of her harlot's hire, and her profits will be used to finance harlotry in a foreign land. This is poetic justice from the righteous, avenging God.

Israel's harlotry is all the more serious because she is Jehovah's wife. The nation as a whole, both the northern and the southern kingdoms, is called Jehovah's spouse, just as the church today is called the bride of Christ. God will judge the church that goes a-whoring from him.

Israel imagined that being Jehovah's wife gave her privilege without responsibility. But Jehovah threatened severe judgment on his prostitute wife: that judgment came in 722 BC when Samaria fell and again in 586 BC when Jerusalem fell. Today, the church is called adulterers and adulteresses when she loves the world (James 4:4) and when she goes after false christs, false gospels, and false spirits (2 Cor. 11:1–4).

Samaria and the northern kingdom are judged first, but Micah's preaching is primarily to Judah. Judah will be judged also: "Therefore shall Zion for your sake be plowed as a field, and

Jerusalem shall become heaps, and the mountain of the house as the high places of the forest" (Mic. 3:12).

Micah teaches this in chapter 1:5: "What are the high places of Judah? Are they not Jerusalem?" Jerusalem, the holy city where Jehovah dwells, is the high places of Judah. The high places were private shrines that the Jews set up to worship God or idols. These places were on every hill and under every green tree, the prophets complained. But the point is that these places were unauthorized and not in the temple. Even Jerusalem itself was given over to idolatry. Moreover, Jehovah would tread upon the high places, which includes Jerusalem. Jerusalem was spared only one hundred and fifty years longer than Israel.

But what of us, and what of the faithful remnant in Israel and Judah? Did Micah have no good news for them? In fact, he did, but not yet in his prophecy. The prophets do not bring the good news until they have thoroughly humbled the people. Micah will give a glorious vision of the future, but we must wait.

There is only one place where a more terrifying judgment has taken place than the one described here, only one mountain where Jehovah's wrath has been poured out with fiercer intensity than here, and that is Calvary. The same wrath, which causes the mountains to melt like wax before the fire, fell upon Christ on the cross. That is why he had to be both God and a perfect, sinless man. For what mere man could withstand the mountain-melting wrath of God? Christ stood in that place of wrath for us, we who believe in him. So when judgment comes, as it will, we must find comfort in the cross. We must repent and flee to Calvary, the one mountain where we will be able to stand.

Chapter 2

Micah's Lament over the Cities of Judah

8. Therefore I will wail and howl, I will go stripped and naked: I will make a wailing like the dragons, and mourning as the owls.
9. For her wound is incurable; for it is come unto Judah; he is come unto the gate of my people, even to Jerusalem.
10. Declare ye it not at Gath, weep ye not at all: in the house of Aphrah roll thyself in the dust.
11. Pass ye away, thou inhabitant of Saphir, having thy shame naked: the inhabitant of Zaanan came not forth in the mourning of Bethezel; he shall receive of you his standing.
12. For the inhabitant of Maroth waited carefully for good: but evil came down from the Lord unto the gate of Jerusalem.
13. O thou inhabitant of Lachish, bind the chariot to the swift beast: she is the beginning of the sin to the daughter of Zion: for the transgressions of Israel were found in thee.
14. Therefore shalt thou give presents to Moreshethgath: the houses of Achzib shall be a lie to the kings of Israel.

15. Yet will I bring an heir unto thee, O inhabitant of Mareshah: he shall come unto Adullam the glory of Israel.
16. Make thee bald, and poll thee for thy delicate children; enlarge thy baldness as the eagle; for they are gone into captivity from thee. (Micah 1:8–16)

In Micah's day, God's people had sinned so grievously that they provoked God to come out of his temple in judgment against them. Micah begins with a vision of the incomparable power and holiness of God. Descending out of his holy place, Jehovah causes the mountains to melt before him; and Samaria, the capital of the northern kingdom of Israel, faces judgment first.

But Judah, the southern kingdom with Jerusalem as its capital, must not be smug, because judgment follows swiftly upon her also. Micah's prophecy is one of incomparable judgment followed by incomparable mercy. Micah prophesies Jerusalem's destruction, her chastisement, her restoration, and her blessedness in the messianic age. But by "Jerusalem" the prophets do not mean the earthly city: they mean the true Jerusalem, God's people, the church.

Jerusalem is the Old Testament type of the church, which is the new or heavenly Jerusalem. Earthly, carnal Jerusalem must be cleansed by judgment to make way for the New Jerusalem. That is what we need to bear in mind as we read through the prophets.

Also, Micah's prophecies do not come in any kind of strict chronological order. That is simply not the prophetic style of the Old Testament. We know that the combined reigns of Jotham, Ahaz, and Hezekiah were sixty-one years. But we do not know, for example, who reigned in Judah when Micah wrote chapter 1 or chapter 2; nor do we need to know. Therefore, we do not know exactly how some of these prophecies were fulfilled. Many of them are best taken as general judgments that include several events. But we do know that the judgments were dreadful, for we see that in the behavior of the prophet himself.

FITTING JUDGMENT

Having announced judgment on Samaria, Micah is given a very painful task. He must prophesy judgment upon his own neighbors, the cities of Judah. The ten cities named in our text are utterly foreign to us, but they were very familiar to Micah.

These cities were cities of defense in Judah near the city of Jerusalem. Various kings had fortified these cities, and they served as protection for the capital. For example, Rehoboam, Judah's first king, fortified Adullam, Mareshah, and Lachish (2 Chron. 11:5–12); and later Jehoshaphat and Jotham did the same (chapters 17 and 27). These cities are therefore representative of Judah's defense: if they fall, what of the rest of the nation of Judah?

The time of the fulfillment of Micah's prophecy is not entirely certain. Since he prophesied during the reigns of three kings, the most likely fulfillment is during the reign of Hezekiah. The prophecy appears to have been fulfilled after the fall of Samaria. At the very least, Samaria's sin was a factor in the judgment that fell on these ten cities. This judgment does not include Jerusalem itself: it comes up to the gate of Jerusalem, but at that point Jehovah's hand is stayed (Mic. 1:9).

In Hezekiah's day, the king of Assyria, Sennacherib, attacked Judah: "Now in the fourteenth year of king Hezekiah did Sennacherib king of Assyria come up against all the fenced cities of Judah, and took them" (2 Kings 18:13). One of the cities that Sennacherib took was Lachish, from which he sent a message to Hezekiah. At that time, Jerusalem was spared only because God killed 185,000 Assyrians in one night!

But the prophets are never neat in their prophecies. This is no criticism of the prophets, but a characteristic of prophetic revelation. The prophets conflate (combine or fuse together) two or more events in one prophecy. This prophecy includes the future deportation of all the Jews. Verse 16 speaks of this: "Poll thee for thy delicate children…for they are gone into captivity from thee." It is best, therefore, to take this prophecy as representative of the many judgments that fall upon the unfaithful nation. Men, women, and children were deported under the Assyrians, Babylonians, and even Egyptians at various times in Israel's history.

Micah describes the judgment of God using a poetic device known as word play. Word play is very effective for evoking certain emotions, but it is very difficult to translate into a foreign language such as English. We can divide the word play into three different categories.

First, with some of the cities the name foreshadows the judgment itself. Beth-le-Aphrah means "house of Aphrah," or house of dust; *Aphrah* in Hebrew means "dust." "In the house of Aphrah roll thyself in the dust" (Mic. 1:10). Rolling in dust was a sign of deep mourning, lamentation, and humiliation. Therefore, a translation that brings out the sense would be: "Dust Town, roll in the dust!"

Bethezel means "house of taking away." "In the mourning of Bethezel; he shall receive of you his standing" (v. 11). The "standing" is the place of standing or the place of protection, support, or standing ground. Bethezel will have nowhere to stand and will cry bitterly. "The mourning of Taking Away Town shall be: 'He has taken away the standing place!'" captures the meaning.

Maroth means "bitterness." "The inhabitant of Maroth waited carefully for good: but evil came down from the LORD" (v. 12). The translation "waited carefully" is very mild. The Hebrew means to "writhe in pain." Maroth expected good to come, perhaps from Jerusalem or from one of the other towns, but no good came, only evil or bitterness. And so Maroth writhed in pain, waiting in vain for some kind of deliverance. "Bitterness came to Bitter Town" is a very rough paraphrase.

Moresheth-gath was Micah's hometown, for he was a Morasthite. "Therefore shalt thou give presents to Moresheth-gath" (v. 14). The presents of verse 14 are parting gifts or gifts given to one who is being sent away. A good translation is "dowry," for the name *Moresheth* comes from the Hebrew for "bride." The meaning is that Moresheth will be sent away with a large dowry, a tribute price. "You will send Bride Town away with a heavy dowry price" captures the significance of Micah's words.

Achzib in Hebrew means "deception." "The houses of Achzib shall be a lie to the kings of Israel" (v. 14). Jeremiah 15:18 asks, "Wilt thou be altogether unto me as a liar, and as waters that fail?" Achzib will be like a lying brook, a stream that dries up just as one needs to drink from it. Achzib's defenses will prove worthless when they are most needed. "Deception Town shall be deception unto the kings of Israel" brings out the sense.

In Hebrew *Lachish* rhymes with *Rachish*, which is the Hebrew word for "chariot." "O thou inhabitant of Lachish, bind the chariot to the swift beast" (v. 13). About Lachish we know the most. It was one of the five cities against which Joshua fought in Joshua 10. King Rehoboam fortified it (2 Chron. 11). Amaziah fled there but was captured and put to death there (chapter 25:27–28). Sennacherib conquered it and made it his base from which to send insulting and blasphemous messages to Hezekiah in Jerusalem (chapter 32). Lachish was a very proud, militarily advanced city. In that day, swift horses and chariots were at the cutting edge of military technology. The irony was that Lachish would bind her chariots to swift horses in order to flee. "Chariot Town shall flee in chariots" is a paraphrase of the meaning.

Second, with some cities the name of the city contrasts with its future judgment. This is the poetic use of irony.

Saphir means "beauty" in Hebrew. "Pass ye away, thou inhabitant of Saphir, having thy shame naked" (Mic. 1:11). The play on words is by way of contrast. Saphir will be stripped of her beauty and will be humiliated:

> 24. And it shall come to pass, that instead of sweet smell there shall be stink; and instead of a girdle a rent; and instead of well set hair baldness; and instead of a stomacher a girding of sackcloth; and burning instead of beauty.
> 25. Thy men shall fall by the sword, and thy mighty in the war.
> 26. And her gates shall lament and mourn; and she being desolate shall sit upon the ground. (Isa. 3:24–26)

> So shall the king of Assyria lead away the Egyptians prisoners, and the Ethiopians captives, young and old, naked and barefoot, even with their buttocks uncovered, to the shame of Egypt" (20:4).

"Beauty Town, pass away in shameful nakedness" captures the meaning here.

Zaanan means "to go out" or "to come forth": "The inhabitant of Zaanan came not forth" (Mic. 1:11). Despite the meaning of her name, Zaanan shall not come forth. She shall be too terrified to come forth and shall cower behind her walls, but to no avail. "Going Out Town shall not come out" brings out the sense.

Mareshah means "possession." "Yet will I bring an heir unto thee, O inhabitant of Mareshah" (v. 15). The heir in verse 15 is one who takes possession or one who dispossesses, that is, a conqueror or invader, such as Sennacherib of Assyria. "I will bring a dispossessor to Possession Town" is a rough paraphrase.

The third category is not so much a play on words from the meaning of the name or poetic irony based on a contrast with the name, but it involves a description alluding to some form of judgment from Israel's history.

Adullam features in the history of David before he was king, when he fled the persecution of Saul. "He shall come unto Adullam the glory of Israel" (v. 15). At one of the lowest points of David's life, he was forced to hide in the caves of Adullam. Adullam will be humiliated once again. The glory of Israel in verse 15 refers to the nobles, the power, and the wealth of the nation. This also comes out in verse 10, "Declare ye it not at Gath." Gath as a Philistine city at this point in history was no more. But verse 10 echoes David's lament in 2 Samuel 1, where he mourns the death of Saul and Jonathan.

There are certain places whose names simply evoke the memory of defeat and humiliation. God's judgment on the cities of Judah will be a second humiliation. We might say, echoing the history of Napoleon, "We will meet our Waterloo." Waterloo was the place for Napoleon's humiliating defeat. Or we might use the example of General Custer's last stand at the Battle of Little Bighorn. "Judah will have her last stand…and fall."

The only positive aspect to this whole prophecy is that Jerusalem itself is spared—for now: "He is come unto the gate of my people, even to Jerusalem" (v. 9). "Evil came down from the LORD unto the gate of Jerusalem" (v. 12).

Notice too that Micah attributes this coming disaster (this "evil") to Jehovah. In this there is judgment, but also hope. If Jehovah is directing the judgment, then his hand can be stayed; there is always room for God's people to repent, for there is always the possibility that in his wrath Jehovah will remember mercy (Hab. 3:2). Micah will remind the people in chapter 7 that Jehovah delights to show mercy to the one who repents, and that is because of his promise to send Jesus Christ.

TERRIBLE SIN

The two sins that especially stand out in our text as the reason for God's judgment are idolatry and (closely related) misplaced confidence.

We know this because the sins of the cities of Judah are the same as the sins of Israel and Samaria. The sins of God's people are sins against the first table of the law. God is angry with his own people (his church) because of their false worship. God has given them the temple in Jerusalem as a token of his gracious presence. The priesthood of Levi and the sacrifices of atonement are there, but the people insist on worshiping God according to their own fancies in their "high places."

The inspired records of Kings and Chronicles give us the three main reasons for Judah's eventual fall. First, idolatry: Judah worshiped other gods or worshiped the true God in an unauthorized manner. Second, impenitence: Judah refused to heed the prophets. Third, Sabbath breaking: Judah would not honor the Sabbath. God therefore gave the land seventy years of rest (ten sabbaths of years).

The other great sin of Judah was her confidence in military power and especially in alliances with other nations. This is very possibly the sin of Lachish mentioned in Micah 1:13. Lachish had her chariots and swift horses, but she trusted in them instead of God. When Lachish and the rest of Judah did this, God displayed to them the impotence of the military in which they placed their hope. Lachish and Judah forgot what she sang in the worship of God: "Some trust in chariots, and some in horses: but we will remember the name of the LORD our God" (Ps. 20:7).

The church of the New Testament is guilty of the same sins and will suffer similar judgment. One of the great controversies that God has with the church is her idolatry. Christians, of course, do not bow down to wood and stone, but Christians trust in money, in power, and in other things besides God. The church is filled with idolatry, from idolizing men and women of fame, to idolizing sports and music, to idolizing preachers and theologians.

The church also has adopted in many places a worship "free for all." Few care today about how God will be worshiped; many imagine they can worship God by bypassing Christ. God is incensed by this. The church today is no more interested in heeding the word of God than Micah's contemporaries were interested in hearing and heeding his message. Many in the church claim to be Christians based on a supposed religious or spiritual experience, but they are not willing to be ruled by scripture. Scripture must not tell them how they will live. But God will not recognize as his children men and women who refuse to hear his word. Let no one deceive you by any means. One who lives for the world and adds some Christian veneer to it is as far from the kingdom of God as is the most abandoned pagan and will be judged more harshly.

The source of Judah's sin was Samaria. In reference to Samaria, God says in Micah 1:9, "Her wound is incurable; for it is come unto Judah; he is come unto the gate of my people, even to Jerusalem." The wound is the heavy blow of judgment with which God has smitten Israel. That wound is both heavy and without any remedy. Indeed, the only remedy is repentance, but since Samaria refused to repent, judgment is inevitable.

But worse than that, Samaria's wound is infectious. The only remedy was amputation of the infectious wound, but Samaria's amputation had come too late: the disease had already spread to

Judah. The way in which sin had spread into Judah from Israel was through Lachish. Verse 13 says, "She is the beginning of the sin to the daughter of Zion."

We do not know how this came about: how were the transgressions of Israel found in Lachish? Did the Israelites bring idolatry to Lachish by means of trade; did some of the men of Lachish visit Samaria and bring back her idolatrous ideas? Possibly, since Lachish was proud and confident, she was more prone to fall into idolatry. She already trusted in her chariots and horses. Also, certain kings were responsible for the spread of infection. Jehoshaphat even formed a close alliance with the house of Ahab. Although Hezekiah did his best to remove idolatry from the nation, his reforms did not last because his own son, Manasseh, undid all his work.

The lesson we learn from this is the danger of the corrupting influence of sin. Israel corrupted Judah, but Judah did not reform Israel. The same is true today: the world corrupts the church, but the church never redeems the world. There are people today who are trying to redeem the world for Christ—they are trying to Christianize politics, entertainment, and education. They seek to do this by cooperating with the ungodly, and they appeal to the notion of common grace. Their efforts are doomed from the start. All they will ever achieve is to bring worldliness into the church, and in so doing they will sow the seeds of the church's destruction. Her wound is incurable!

The greatest corrupting influence in the world today is the false church. Israel was not the world; Assyria and Babylon were the world. Israel was the false church. Israel was the world with God written on it. That is the false church. But God disowned Israel: he called her a harlot, and through the prophet Hosea he even says to her, "Ye are not my people" (Hos. 1:9). The only answer to the corruption of the world and the false church is not cooperation, but the calling of her to repentance and the calling of individuals out of her to worship in the true church. We need to be very careful about the kind of people we meet, the kind of friends we have, and the kind of things we watch, read, or look at online, because the world and the false church are as infectious as the plague.

BITTER MOURNING

In response to the destruction of Samaria and to the destruction of Judah's cities, Micah laments bitterly. Micah's lament is public, loud, and visible: this will make an impression on Judah.

If you were in Judah you would have seen an unusually dressed prophet. Micah went around stripped and naked (Mic. 1:8). This does not mean that Micah wore no clothes, but that he removed his outer clothing. Micah was not the only prophet to behave like this:

2. At the same time spake the Lord by Isaiah the son of Amoz, saying, Go and loose the sackcloth from off thy loins, and put off thy shoe from thy foot. And he did so, walking naked and barefoot.
3. And the Lord said, Like as my servant Isaiah hath walked naked and barefoot three years for a sign and wonder upon Egypt and upon Ethiopia;
4. So shall the king of Assyria lead away the Egyptians prisoners, and the Ethiopians captives, young and old, naked and barefoot, even with their buttocks uncovered, to the shame of Egypt. (Isa. 20:2–4)

Micah's clothing is that not only of a mourner at a funeral, but of a captive. Micah explains his behavior in chapter 1:16: "for they are gone into captivity from thee." Micah wears the clothing of a prisoner of war, therefore, because he foresees that his nation of Israel and Judah will be taken away as prisoners of war (Isa. 3:24). Perhaps if a prophet wore an orange jumpsuit, we would get a similar idea today.

Added to this visual display, the clothing of humiliation and defeat, Micah cries. If you had been there, you would have seen an unusually dressed prophet walking up and down in the streets of Jerusalem and Judah wailing with a loud voice, and that would have made quite an impression upon you. Micah describes his wailing like two kinds of animals familiar to the people of his day. The words are difficult to translate, but the most likely candidates are not dragons and owls, but jackals and eagle owls or even ostriches.

One commentator writes of the jackal, "The jackals make a lamentable howling noise, so that travelers unacquainted with them would think that a company of people, women or children, were howling, one to another."[1] About the ostrich he writes, "Its screech is spoken of by travelers as 'fearful, affrighting.' 'During the lonesome part of the night they often make a doleful and piteous noise. I have often heard them groan, as if they were in the greatest agonies.'"[2]

Micah calls his fellow countrymen to join him in his bitter lamentation. Aphrah he calls to roll about in dust; Bethezel mourns; Maroth writhes in agony. He ends with a call to them to pull their hair out in great bitterness, to make their heads bald like the vulture. But let not the mourning and lamentation be heard by Gath, the enemy. All of this speaks of the great tragedy that is coming: the judgment is inevitable, the judgment will be dreadful, and Micah himself is moved to weep over it.

---

1 E. B. Pusey, *The Minor Prophets, A Commentary Explanatory and Practical*, vol. 2 (repr., Grand Rapids, MI: Baker Book House, 1974), 21.
2 Ibid.

Do you ever weep over the sins of the church? We should be moved to confess what David did in Psalm 119:136: "Rivers of waters run down mine eyes, because they keep not thy law." We should identify with weeping Jeremiah: "But if ye will not hear it, my soul shall weep in secret places for your pride; and mine eyes shall weep sore, and run down with tears, because the LORD's flock is carried away captive" (Jer. 13:17). We should have the sentiment of Paul: "I have great heaviness and continual sorrow in my heart" (Rom. 9:2).

Micah identifies himself with Judah and weeps over her destruction. He does not stand afar off and gloat over it. This must be the same for the preacher today whose love for the church must drive him to tears. That destruction is because Judah has rejected the only salvation in Jesus Christ. Without repentance and faith in the crucified Jesus, a worse judgment of God is coming, the judgment of eternal damnation.

Let us flee from our sins and find our salvation in Jesus Christ, and in the final judgment we will be able to stand.

Chapter 3

Woe to the Inheritance Dispossessors!

1. Woe to them that devise iniquity, and work evil upon their beds! when the morning is light, they practise it, because it is in the power of their hand.
2. And they covet fields, and take them by violence; and houses, and take them away: so they oppress a man and his house, even a man and his heritage.
3. Therefore thus saith the Lord; Behold, against this family do I devise an evil, from which ye shall not remove your necks; neither shall ye go haughtily: for this time is evil.
4. In that day shall one take up a parable against you, and lament with a doleful lamentation, and say, We be utterly spoiled: he hath changed the portion of my people: how hath he removed it from me! turning away he hath divided our fields.
5. Therefore thou shalt have none that shall cast a cord by lot in the congregation of the Lord...
8. Even of late my people is risen up as an enemy: ye pull off the robe with the garment from them that pass by securely as men averse from war.

9. The women of my people have ye cast out from their pleasant houses; from their children have ye taken away my glory for ever.

10. Arise ye, and depart; for this is not your rest: because it is polluted, it shall destroy you, even with a sore destruction. (Micah 2:1–5, 8–10)

We must remember when studying the prophets that they address the people of God. Therefore, we must apply their teachings to the church and not to society in general. Remember that in the Old Testament the church and the nation were one. Micah knew nothing about a separation of religious and social affairs. Micah also knew of only one place where God ruled over his people by his word and Spirit, and that place was Israel or the land of Canaan.

Micah boldly confronts the people of Israel, especially in this chapter the rich and powerful, for their sins. In chapter 1, he had not made any specific applications to sin. He spoke of high places in Judah and spiritual whoredom in Samaria. In chapter 2, Micah exposes sins against the second table of God's law, especially the eighth and tenth commandments, against theft and covetousness.

In this chapter, he addresses the sins of the people regarding property. Israel was an agrarian society: the people lived and worked on the land and relied upon simple agriculture for their needs. We live in a different time, the industrial and information age. In an agrarian society, land was very important to the Israelite, and it was a valuable resource. Men with land grew crops and sold them for profit. Therefore, it was disastrous for a man in Israel to be deprived of his land.

In chapter 2, Micah condemns greedy landowners who stole the land from others. This was wicked oppression of the neighbor, the activity of an enemy (v. 8). But more than that, this was the theft of the land of Canaan, the holy land that God had given to his people as a gracious inheritance. That is the main idea of our text: the oppression of a man in his inheritance. Not land as such, but inheritance, is the issue here. That explains the terrible woe.

THE PRECIOUS INHERITANCE

Micah 2 is about houses, lands, and fields, but not just any houses, lands, and fields. The issue in Micah 2 is inheritance, a particular type of property.

The proof of this is found in the chapter itself. Verse 2 speaks of "a man and his heritage" (heritage is inheritance). Verse 4 speaks of "the portion of my people," and verse 5 speaks of "cast[ing] a cord by lot in the congregation of the LORD" (this refers to the apportioning or sharing out of the inheritance). Verse 9 speaks of "pleasant houses" and "glory" (a reference to the richness of the inheritance), and verse 10 speaks about "rest" (the enjoyment of the inheritance).

An inheritance is a gracious gift received by children from their father. It is not earned, and it is certainly not stolen. Rather, it is passed down from father to son. The inheritance of Micah 2 is the inheritance of the land of Canaan, the land that Israel received by inheritance from God himself. That inheritance was promised to Abraham and his seed long before Abraham's descendants ever came into possession of it. God gave Israel her inheritance by redeeming her from Egypt, preserving her through the wilderness, and fighting her battles in the days of Joshua. Ever since Joshua, Jehovah preserved and maintained that inheritance.

In Israel each Israelite family received his own inheritance, his own part of the land. The exact portion was determined by lot, which was the way in which Joshua discerned God's will. This was done by "cast[ing] a cord" (v. 5). Where the line fell, that was the inheritance. There was to be no fighting or rivalry among the tribes, for God gave each person a portion. Perhaps one man received a smaller portion than another. Perhaps he received a less fertile or fruitful plot of ground than his neighbor. Perhaps one man received a portion closer to Jerusalem, or nearer the coast, or in the valleys, or in the mountains. God determined that piece of land for him. Therefore, each Israelite possessed a piece of land (a field, a vineyard, a small farm) on which he lived and worked, and which he could call his own.

Ultimately, however, the land of Canaan belonged to Jehovah: "The land is mine; for ye are strangers and sojourners with me" (Lev. 25:23). The land of Canaan, in a special way, was the dwelling place of God, and he dwelled especially in the temple. There, between the cherubim, atop the mercy seat of the ark, in the holy of holies, Jehovah dwelled. To be in the land of Canaan meant to have a place in the congregation (the gathering, the assembly, even the church) of Jehovah.

This made Canaan unique. No other land in the world could boast of Jehovah's gracious presence in this way. And no land is like Canaan today. Because of all of this, the inheritance of a man in Israel was sacred, sacrosanct. It could not be bought or sold, and it certainly must not be stolen. But that is exactly what was happening in Micah's day.

If the land of Canaan was the land of God's covenant, it was necessary for the salvation of God's people that they enjoy the exact portion allotted to them. In a very real way, the salvation of the Israelites was tied up in their plot of land, their portion of God's inheritance. The portion was a picture, a foretaste, a foreshadowing of the eternal portion in the heavenly Canaan. Each elect child of God enjoyed his salvation exactly in the place where God positioned him and nowhere else. He was not at liberty to change his portion. Each believer had his own place in the kingdom, it had been allotted to him in particular, and God willed that he enjoy salvation there:

8. By faith Abraham, when he was called to go out into a place which he should after receive for an inheritance, obeyed; and he went out, not knowing whither he went.

9. By faith he sojourned in the land of promise, as in a strange country, dwelling in tabernacles with Isaac and Jacob, the heirs with him of the same promise:

10. For he looked for a city which hath foundations, whose builder and maker is God...

14. For they that say such things declare plainly that they seek a country.

15. And truly, if they had been mindful of that country from whence they came out, they might have had opportunity to have returned.

16. But now they desire a better country, that is, an heavenly: wherefore God is not ashamed to be called their God: for he hath prepared for them a city (Heb. 11:8–10, 14–16).

The portion, therefore, although a physical plot of ground in a certain geographical location, was of great spiritual significance. The believer's portion, whether in the Old Testament or New Testament, is God himself (see Ps. 16:5–6) or, better, God in Jesus Christ. And the people themselves were Jehovah's inheritance (Mic. 7:14, 18). Our inheritance in Jesus Christ is the reality of which the believer's Old Testament portion was a type.

Christ was promised to the Israelites. They saw him; they enjoyed him; they longed for him; they trusted in him. And the cross was the basis of all of this. This was true, of course, only of true Israel, of the elect within the nation. The reprobate, ungodly, unbelieving Israelites received only land, but with it they did not receive God's covenantal blessings.

There is a striking example of this in 1 Kings 21, where a humble, saintly Israelite peasant refused to sell his vineyard to unbelieving, wicked King Ahab. Naboth received what appears to be a reasonable offer of exchange. Naboth had a vineyard next to Ahab's summer palace, but Ahab wanted Naboth's vineyard so that he could build a garden of herbs. Ahab said to Naboth in verse 2, "Give me thy vineyard." Naboth's refusal is decisive: "The LORD forbid it me, that I should give the inheritance of my fathers unto thee" (v. 3). Naboth evaluates his vineyard very differently than Ahab does. Ahab sees a potential garden; Naboth sees the inheritance of his fathers. Naboth's fathers handed that inheritance to him, and he was under divine obligation to hand it down to his children. Therefore, he would not sell. He remembered God's word in Leviticus 25:23: "The land shall not be sold forever."

Nevertheless, the law did make provision for the poor, who could temporarily allow someone else to possess the land (Lev. 25:10, 13–17, 25–28). The point is that, however a portion might temporarily change hands, it had to be restored to its original owners. These laws guaranteed that each family would retain the portion allotted to them by God. Ahab did not care about God's law: he murdered Naboth and his sons and stole the vineyard. God later avenged Naboth's blood.

In the Old Testament there were two kinds of Israelites: those who enjoyed salvation typically in the plot of land allotted to them and those who enjoyed the type (the land) without possessing the reality. Ahab had a portion of land too, and as king he increased his fields and vineyards, but he did not have the reality. He was an Israelite in name only. Naboth enjoyed salvation in his vineyard, and when he was cruelly murdered he entered into the enjoyment of his inheritance in heaven.

The same is true today except that the spiritual inheritance we enjoy is not at all tied to a specific piece of ground. We can enjoy salvation anywhere. What we have in the New Testament is richer, better, and greater than anything the Old Testament saints ever enjoyed in their portion in Canaan. The New Testament makes clear that all the promises of blessing to Abraham and his seed belong to all Christians, who are the seed of Abraham. The blessings of the Old Testament were real: peace with God, covenantal fellowship, eternal righteousness, joy in the Holy Spirit, forgiveness of sins, and eternal life. But we have them in a greater fullness because we live after the cross and after Pentecost. All these blessings are ours because Jesus Christ died on the cross to purchase them. They were all promised in the Old Testament, but they could not be received until the one in whose name the promises were made came and made atonement:

> If children, then heirs; heirs of God, and joint-heirs with Christ; if so be that we suffer with him, that we may be also glorified together. (Rom. 8:17)

> If ye be Christ's, then are ye Abraham's seed, and heirs according to the promise. (Gal. 3:29)

> In whom also we have obtained an inheritance, being predestinated according to the purpose of him who worketh all things after the counsel of his own will. (Eph. 1:11)

> For this cause he is the mediator of the new testament, that by means of death, for the redemption of the transgressions that were under the first testament, they which are called might receive the promise of eternal inheritance. (Heb. 9:15)

To an inheritance incorruptible, and undefiled, and that fadeth not away, reserved in heaven for you. (1 Pet. 1:4)

THE CRUEL DISPOSSESSION

If we understand that spiritual reality of the land of Canaan, we will understand the sin condemned in the passage before us. It is not mere oppression or theft, but it is a robbing of a fellow Israelite of his inheritance. The sin of these men is so serious because it is a sin against God's covenantal people. Robbery and oppression are awful, but robbing your own brethren is an especially heinous crime against God.

Micah traces the development of their sin. First, they covet: "they covet fields" (Mic. 2:2). For these men it is not enough that God has given each of them a plot in Canaan. They do not sing, "The LORD is the portion of mine inheritance and of my cup: thou maintainest my lot. The lines are fallen unto me in pleasant places; yea, I have a goodly heritage" (Ps. 16:5–6). Of them the words of Isaiah 5:8 are true: "Woe unto them that join house to house, that lay field to field, till there be no place, that they may be placed alone in the midst of the earth!" Insatiably greedy, these men desire the fields and houses (the inheritance) of others.

Second, they devise a scheme to acquire what they covet: "Woe to them that devise iniquity, and work evil upon their beds!" (Mic. 2:1). When others are sleeping, these men are plotting: how can I get my hands on my neighbor's house, field, land, or property? But notice that God in heaven knows about their secret plotting. This must have come as a rude awakening to these greedy men.

Third, they seize the inheritance of others: "They…take them by violence…and take them away…they oppress a man" (v. 2). Micah does not explain their methods; some of it may have been simple robbery, but much of it was done under the appearance of legality. As we shall see later, the judges of Israel were corrupt, so these greedy men succeeded in oppressing their neighbors, evicting families, and stealing inheritances. Verse 8 describes their cruel and despicable activity: "Even of late my people is risen up as an enemy."

The victims of these men were not the poor, for the poor had nothing worth stealing. They were Israelites with property, and after these men were finished their victims were poor, even destitute. In that day, if a man lost his portion in Canaan, he was reduced to servitude or begging. These men were opportunists: they preyed on the vulnerable. Their victims were men (v. 2), women and children (vv. 9–10, and in the absence of men they were probably widows and orphans), and even innocent passersby (v. 8).

Verse 8 describes the scene: "them that pass by securely as men averse from war." The idea is of men who did not suspect anything. The last thing they expected was to be robbed by their own people. That they were "as men averse from war" means either that they were peaceful people (turning from war, no fighters) or that they were returning from war. They expected as returning from battle to be safe and secure in Jerusalem.

Crimes against widows and orphans and stripping a man of his robe (vv. 8–10) were particularly heinous crimes. Widows and orphans were especially protected by the law of Moses (Ex. 22:22–24; Deut. 27:19). The reference to a robe might be a literal description of what was happening, or it might be an expression of how rapacious these men were. They would rip the shirt from a man's back. There was a law against taking a man's outer garment (Ex. 22:25–27; Deut. 24:10–13). All of this paints these men in a terrible light. God knows about their sins and will severely judge them.

How do we apply this? Do we take this as mere social commentary? Do the minor prophets have an anti-poverty, pro-socialism, social justice message that the church needs to promote today? That is the view of many Christians. They want the church to act as a prophetic voice against poverty, and they want the church to address social inequality.

But that is not the point of Micah or of the prophets in general. The minor prophets do not offer a socialist manifesto to help the downtrodden. The prophets address sin *in the church*: here the prophet addresses the issues of inheritance, of hatred for the neighbor, of despising of God's commandments. But we do not have a theocracy today, one nation that is God's people, with laws about land, fields, and houses or laws about cloaks.

The New Testament church never made political application in the apostolic age. None of the apostles ever used the prophets as a reason to address societal ills. The apostles preached about sin in the church; they taught the gospel; and they taught that the gospel produces a different kind of life, a life in which believers will not defraud one another (1 Thess. 4:6). Christians who are guilty of oppressing one another or stealing from one another must be placed under discipline and called to repentance.

It is necessary when studying Old Testament typology to discover the point of comparison and the failure of the type. Every type must fail to make way for the reality. That is why the land of Canaan itself had to fail.

If there are those in the church today who are guilty of the sins described here, they must be found among those who seek to steal our inheritance. Our inheritance is not the land of Canaan: we do not need to be concerned with people stealing our vineyards or driving us from our houses. Our inheritance is the truth of the gospel, at the center of which is the truth of Christ crucified. Those who subvert *that* are the inheritance dispossessors today. Ironically, it is those who corrupt scripture and who preach a different gospel, one without Christ crucified, who are the ones who try to steal our inheritance.

Unlike the land of Canaan, which could be and was stolen from Israel and which was eventually delivered into the hands of the Babylonians, our inheritance is secure. Naboth could lose his vineyard and even his life because of Ahab's wickedness, but he did not and could not lose his salvation in Christ. All the men of Judah could and did lose their fields, vineyards, and houses when the Babylonians came, but no true Israelite who believes in Jesus Christ (whether from the Jews or Gentiles) can lose the forgiveness of sins, fellowship with God, joy in the Holy Spirit, peace with God, and eternal life purchased for us by the blood of the Savior. As Peter writes, our inheritance is "incorruptible, and undefiled, and that fadeth not away, reserved in heaven for you" (1 Pet. 1:4).

THE RIGHTEOUS JUDGMENT

God's judgment is to disinherit the dispossessors, a judgment that fits the crime. These wicked men dispossessed God's people; therefore, God dispossesses them. In Micah 2:1, they devise iniquity, and in verse 3, Jehovah devises evil against them. This does not mean that Jehovah sins; the evil of verse 3 is calamity or disaster. This evil will take the form of bondage: God will place a yoke upon their necks. That yoke is the coming Assyrian and Babylonian captivities. The judgment of God will be inescapable ("from which ye shall not remove your necks," v. 3).

In verse 9, these men cast women and children out of their homes; in verse 10, Jehovah casts them out of their homes and sends them away. In verse 10, the words, "Arise ye, and depart," are probably the words of these evil men to defenseless widows and orphans. Now God says to these men, "Get out!" When they die, God will say to them, "Depart from me, ye cursed, into everlasting fire, prepared for the devil and his angels" (Matt. 25:41).

In chapter 2:10, Micah adds the reason: "because it is polluted." Pollution here is ceremonial and moral uncleanness or defilement. The presence of these wicked men has defiled the land of Canaan. These men have no place there. Instead, they must be utterly destroyed, in Babylon and then in hell. The reason is that these men are reprobate within the elect nation. They have no part in the congregation of Jehovah, and when there is a future restoration, they will have no portion in it (alluded to in v. 5). The land of Canaan, even as they greedily gather as much of it to themselves as they can at the expense of their neighbors, is not their rest (v. 10). They do not experience fellowship in the covenant with Jehovah there.

The effect of this judgment is bitter lamentation, the wailing of despair. "We be utterly spoiled" (v. 4) (or, "Ruined! We are ruined!") God himself predicts their lamentation, which will be used as a parable against them. The idea is that it will be used in mockery by their captors. It will be galling to see the Babylonians take the lands, fields, and houses that these men had spent their days accumulating for themselves. The galling character comes out in verse 4: "Turning away he hath divided our fields," or more literally, "How he hath removed from me to the one turning back." The one turning back is the apostate or the backslider: here it means the captors. This is surely a fitting judgment for those who never appreciated their inheritance in the land: it will be taken away from them, and they will be cut off in their generations.

But the faithful, even the dispossessed in this world, will never lose their true, spiritual inheritance, for that inheritance is safe in Jesus Christ.

Chapter 4

Micah Told To Stop Preaching

6. Prophesy ye not, say they to them that prophesy: they shall not prophesy to them, that they shall not take shame.

7. O thou that art named the house of Jacob, is the spirit of the Lord straitened? are these his doings? do not my words do good to him that walketh uprightly?...

11. If a man walking in the spirit and falsehood do lie, saying, I will prophesy unto thee of wine and of strong drink; he shall even be the prophet of this people. (Micah 2:6–7, 11)

Micah was not a popular preacher. Although he includes some beautiful prophecies of future hope, he begins by proclaiming judgment. He announces judgment against sin, judgment against sinners, and judgment against Israel and Judah. He threatens specific judgment against particular, named cities. And he threatens judgment because of specific, named sins, sins committed by the people of God.

This is how true preachers must always preach. Before a preacher can preach Christ and the glories of salvation, he must preach sin. The people of the church must know their sin in order to live in thankfulness. This means that the preacher must be detailed and specific when he exposes sin. There is no point in making vague references to sin. Sin must be defined, explained, and condemned, and the minister must not be squeamish about this. He must do it without fear or favor.

In chapter 2, the people begin to object to Micah's message. Micah has deeply offended them, and they make their opposition known. They react, as the wicked always do, by rejecting the word of God.

The rich landowners of chapter 2 have come under Micah's scrutiny. He rebukes them for their cruel dispossession of their neighbor's inheritance. He exposes their secret deals and their violent oppression, even revealing the sins of which they are guilty as they lie upon their beds at night. He prophesies a terrible and humiliating judgment: dispossession by the Babylonians. In modern parlance, Micah prophesies that the wealthy and prominent but wicked church members will have no place in God's church, that God will cut them off with their children and cast them into hell.

But the people are not going to stand for it. Verse 6 comes almost as an indignant interruption to the prophet: "Prophesy ye not. Stop prophesying. Do not prophesy!"

THE PROPHET REJECTED

Prophecy is quite simply the proclamation of the word of God. A prophet might prophesy concerning the past, present, or future, but when he prophesies he brings the word of God. Micah employs the verb *to prophesy*. The literal translation is "to drop," that is, to let words fall as droplets. Four times he uses that verb.

The verb *to drop* with respect to prophesying has both positive and negative connotations. In Deuteronomy 32:2 Moses declares, "My doctrine shall drop as the rain, my speech shall distill as the dew." The imagery is of the refreshment that the word of God brings. But in Proverbs 19:13 we read that "the contentions of a wife are a continual dropping." The imagery there is of the annoying sound of persistent rain. In history, the constant drip, drip of water was even used as a form of torture.

In Micah's day the people viewed his prophesying as a source of irritation, and they wanted it to stop. It was annoying for them to have the constant reminder of their own sins and the constant warning of God's judgment. Thus they say, and Micah echoes them in chapter 2:6, "Prophesy ye not." This was their continual plea to Micah. The translation of verse 6 is, "Do not drop, they drop. They shall not drop," or "Do not prophesy, they prophesy. They shall not prophesy." As Micah constantly and faithfully prophesied, the people constantly and faithlessly called him *not* to prophesy. Micah's hearers could not bear to hear him or any true prophet (notice that it is "prophesy *ye* not," which is plural).

Micah's prophecy was rejected because of its content. It was not that Micah was a lackluster speaker, or that Micah lacked zeal or even empathy with the people. It was that Micah preached sin and judgment to a people who wanted to live in sin without the threat of judgment. Verse 6 states, "They shall not prophesy to them." An alternative translation is, "They shall not prophesy regarding these things."

"O Micah," the people cry, "do not prophesy about these things to us. If you want to preach doom and gloom, preach to others. Preach to the heathen, but do not preach sin and judgment to us."

"O Micah," the people complain, "your message is too negative. You preach judgment against Samaria and the cities of Judah, and even against the rich businessmen of the nation. We do not want to hear such things." Remember the immediate context of "these things" is verses 4–5: God shall take away the fields of Judah and apportion them to the heathen. "Surely not, Micah!"

This is the same reason for the rejection of the preaching today. While the minister is not inspired as was Micah, he brings the word of God, and when he does that faithfully, Christ himself speaks through him. The people will say, "O pastor, you are like a long-playing record. The same message, week in, week out, like the constant drip, drip, drip! Always the same message: God, Jesus, sin." When the people become really fed up with the preaching, they will get rid of the preacher or leave the church so they do not have to hear it any longer, or they will find someone else who will give them a message that they want to hear.

That was the experience of Micah, of Jeremiah, of Isaiah, of every true preacher, and of Jesus Christ himself.

The form of rejection of prophecy varies, but at root it has the same cause: hatred for and rejection of the word of God. This too is a very important factor in God's judgment of Judah: they rejected the prophets.

Sometimes people reject the prophet (and the preaching) by refusing to listen. We can well imagine that the people knew where and when Micah would preach. Many of them simply avoided him. Amos said, "They hate him that rebuketh in the gate, and they abhor him that speaketh uprightly" (Amos 5:10). Do you really imagine that the rich, oppressing landowners of chapter 2 frequented the sermons of Micah the prophet? If they heard him once or twice, they got the message, and since they had no intention of repenting, they also had no intention of continuing to listen.

That is the number-one form of opposition to true preaching today. If I know that the preaching will expose my sin and call me to repent and live a holy life, I simply will avoid it. The conscience of the wicked cannot stand to hear the preaching of the truth. Unbelievers and apostate Christians know where they will hear truth. Therefore, they avoid it. That is why some have left true churches of Jesus Christ. It was not that the sermons were too long or too deep; it was that they were too sharp: they cut too deeply. Then the temptation is for the pastor to water down the truth. By the grace of God, the true preacher has no intention of softening the message. The preacher dare not soften the message, for it is not the preacher's message but God's: "But truly I am full of power by the spirit of the LORD, and of judgment, and of might, to declare unto Jacob his transgression, and to Israel his sin" (Mic. 3:8).

Do not be fooled: an unbeliever who avoids the preaching will be punished by God. Avoiding the preaching does not mean that he will avoid the judgment. Only by repentance and faith can we avoid judgment. Calvin's comments on this text are sharp:

> The wicked and unbelievers consider it a great victory once God ceases to address them. They relax and indulge in good times, for they think that God's judgment will never overtake them, since they no longer hear his threats...When Saint Paul says that vengeance awaits all despisers of God and God's Word, he has no intention of excusing those who simply prefer not to hear the message.[1]

Another way in which the people reject the prophet (and today the preaching) is by forbidding him to preach and by contradicting his message. Micah 2:6 is a prohibition: "Prophesy ye *not*... They shall *not* prophesy" (emphasis added). Do not

---

1 John Calvin, *Sermons on the Book of Micah*, trans. and ed. Benjamin Wirt Farley (Phillipsburg, NJ: P&R Publishing, 2003), 96, 108.

preach! Stop preaching! We will not tolerate preaching like that here! That is always the response of the wicked:

12. Also Amaziah said unto Amos, O thou seer, go, flee thee away into the land of Judah, and there eat bread, and prophesy there:
13. But prophesy not again any more at Bethel: for it is the king's chapel, and it is the king's court. (Amos 7:12–13)

And they called them, and commanded them not to speak at all nor teach in the name of Jesus. (Acts 4:18)

27. And when they had brought them, they set them before the council: and the high priest asked them,
28. Saying, Did not we straitly command you that ye should not teach in this name? and, behold, ye have filled Jerusalem with your doctrine, and intend to bring this man's blood upon us.
29. Then Peter and the other apostles answered and said, We ought to obey God rather than men. (5:27–29)

The true church must continue to preach for the glory of God and the good of God's children even when the powers of the false church and the ungodly state forbid it.

Micah's hearers also opposed him by contradicting the message itself. Micah was mocked, taunted, and reproached as a prophet of doom. Chapter 2:6b, "that they shall not take shame," can be translated in various ways. Literally, the Hebrew reads, "not shall turn away reproaches." There are two possibilities here: either because of Judah's rejection of the word of God the shameful reproach of judgment shall not be averted; or Judah is saying, "Reproaches shall not come. Shame shall not overturn us." The second option fits the context better: Micah has just warned about the shameful taunt of the heathen who will mock Judah when they take her land. Judah's response is to deny the word of God: "Shame shall not come; do not speak that way, Micah!"

The preacher's message is denied as much today as it was in Micah's day, especially if the preacher dares bring God's message of judgment on sin. If you tell the adulterer, even the adulterer in the church, that God will judge him for his adultery, the response is, "No, pastor, shame shall never come." If you tell the crooked businessman, the liar, the thief, the fornicator, the worldly person, or the drunkard that God will not tolerate such sin in his church, you will be called a fanatic or a legalist.

The defense of such a church member is this: "I am a child of God, and I even come to church. God will not judge me for my sins. I accepted Jesus as my savior, and God does not care how I live through the week." That is why many churches, even Reformed churches, tolerate young people who fornicate with their girlfriends, who get drunk and party at the weekends, and who then come to worship on Sunday as if all were well. Jeremiah encountered the same stubborn impenitence in his day:

4. Trust ye not in lying words, saying, The temple of the Lord, The temple of the Lord, The temple of the Lord, are these.
5. For if ye throughly amend your ways and your doings; if ye throughly execute judgment between a man and his neighbour;
6. If ye oppress not the stranger, the fatherless, and the widow, and shed not innocent blood in this place, neither walk after other gods to your hurt:
7. Then will I cause you to dwell in this place, in the land that I gave to your fathers, for ever and ever.
8. Behold, ye trust in lying words, that cannot profit.

9. Will ye steal, murder, and commit adultery, and swear falsely, and burn incense unto Baal, and walk after other gods whom ye know not;

10. And come and stand before me in this house, which is called by my name, and say, We are delivered to do all these abominations?

11. Is this house, which is called by my name, become a den of robbers in your eyes? Behold, even I have seen it, saith the Lord. (Jer. 7:4–11)

THE PROPHET REPLACED

In a verse dripping with irony and sarcasm, Micah describes the prophet whom the people want, a prophet whom they would gladly choose over Micah, the true prophet of the Lord. The ideal prophet for an apostate people is a "prosperity prophet."

In the Old Testament wine and strong drink are not only images of drunkenness, but more particularly here, wine and strong drink mean prosperity without judgment. To have wine and strong drink in Judah means two things: first, there must be a good harvest to produce the grapes and grains necessary to make wine and other drinks; and second, there must be peace in the land so that wine can be produced and enjoyed without the interference of the enemy. Remember that in the Old Testament wine is a symbol of joy, a blessing of God, and that good harvests and peace are seen as blessings upon the land of Canaan. If a man came along and preached *that* message, he would be readily received as a prophet by this people.

Micah would dearly love to preach a prosperity message, but he cannot because God does not bless a disobedient and apostate people. Micah brings the message that God gives and none other. Blessings in scripture come through obedience and faithfulness to God; Judah should have known this. How could they, who defrauded their neighbors, expect blessing? Instead, Micah was called to bring a painful message of judgment, but God would through judgment redeem his people and purify them. Only once the message of judgment had been understood could Micah bring the glorious message of salvation. Only one who understands his sin can receive the message of the forgiveness of sins.

The false and apostate church cannot be satisfied with no preaching. Otherwise, she would be the world. She needs to believe that she has some message from God, so she craves a false prophet to preach a flattering message.

In the modern church, there are the blatantly obvious prosperity preachers such as Joel Osteen, Joyce Meyer, or the aptly named Creflo Dollar. These kinds of preachers simply proclaim the message that God wants all people to be healthy and rich, to have no problems, and to prosper in everything they do. Most of these preachers are fabulously wealthy themselves because their message is very popular with the covetous masses. Jesus becomes a way to get rich.

Oh yes, if a man (or woman) says, "I will prophesy unto thee of prosperity," he or she will be a prophet of this people!

Then there is the preacher who proclaims an "easy believism" message of Christianity, according to which Christianity is not about believing the truth and living a godly life in thanksgiving for God's gracious salvation. Christianity is connecting with God, following Jesus, and being nice. But such churches never specify what it means to follow Jesus, and they usually disparage doctrine and strict godliness.

Oh yes, if a man (or woman) says, "I will prophesy unto thee of an easy relationship with Jesus with no responsibilities," he or she will be a prophet of this people.

Then there is the preacher who makes everything about how

to be a good person, but who never preaches sin or the cross of Jesus Christ. He will be a prophet of this people! Moralistic, pep-talk, entertainment preaching attracts the kind of people Micah repelled. Such people would run a mile if they encountered true preaching.

Micah makes a few important observations about such would-be, popular prophets. First, such a man comes "walking in the spirit" (Mic. 2:11). The KJV translators write "spirit" with a lowercase *s*. This is correct, but in the estimation of the false prophet and the people, the man preaches by the Holy Spirit. The false prophet has to claim that God sent him. Otherwise, he would have no credibility. The people are not going to follow someone who admits that he is a false prophet!

22. Now therefore, behold, the Lord hath put a lying spirit in the mouth of these thy prophets, and the Lord hath spoken evil against thee.
23. Then Zedekiah the son of Chenaanah came near, and smote Micaiah upon the cheek, and said, Which way went the spirit of the Lord from me to speak unto thee? (2 Chron. 18:22–23)

10. Then Hananiah the prophet took the yoke from off the prophet Jeremiah's neck, and brake it.
11. And Hananiah spake in the presence of all the people, saying, Thus saith the Lord; Even so will I break the yoke of Nebuchadnezzar king of Babylon from the neck of all nations within the space of two full years. And the prophet Jeremiah went his way.
12. Then the word of the Lord came unto Jeremiah the prophet, after that Hananiah the prophet had broken the yoke from off the neck of the prophet Jeremiah, saying,

13. Go and tell Hananiah, saying, Thus saith the Lord; Thou hast broken the yokes of wood; but thou shalt make for them yokes of iron.

14. For thus saith the Lord of hosts, the God of Israel; I have put a yoke of iron upon the neck of all these nations, that they may serve Nebuchadnezzar king of Babylon; and they shall serve him: and I have given him the beasts of the field also.

15. Then said the prophet Jeremiah unto Hananiah the prophet, Hear now, Hananiah; The Lord hath not sent thee; but thou makest this people to trust in a lie.

16. Therefore thus saith the Lord; Behold, I will cast thee from off the face of the earth: this year thou shalt die, because thou hast taught rebellion against the Lord.

17. So Hananiah the prophet died the same year in the seventh month. (Jer. 28:10–17)

Second, such a man (or woman) is a liar. The Hebrew emphasizes this with two synonyms ("falsehood" and "lie") in the same verse (Mic. 2:11); and in Hebrew the words *falsehood* and *strong drink* rhyme.

Third, such a man is exactly what the people want and deserve. In fact, when a false preacher deceives the people and they perish, it is their own fault. The false church wants to believe lies; they will not under any circumstances believe the truth. God gives the false church lying prophets as judgment. In this way, he gives them what they want and punishes them for their evil desires:

8. Now go, write it before them in a table, and note it in a book, that it may be for the time to come for ever and ever:

9. That this is a rebellious people, lying children, children that will not hear the law of the Lord:

10. Which say to the seers, See not; and to the prophets, Prophesy not unto us right things, speak unto us
smooth things, prophesy deceits:

11. Get you out of the way, turn aside out of the path,
cause the Holy One of Israel to cease from before us.
(Isa. 30:8–11)

The prophets prophesy falsely, and the priests bear rule
by their means; and my people love to have it so: and
what will ye do in the end thereof? (Jer. 5:31)

My people are destroyed for lack of knowledge: because
thou hast rejected knowledge, I will also reject thee, that
thou shalt be no priest to me: seeing thou hast forgotten the law of thy God, I will also forget thy children.
(Hos. 4:6)

10. And with all deceivableness of unrighteousness in
them that perish; because they received not the love of
the truth, that they might be saved.

11. And for this cause God shall send them strong delusion, that they should believe a lie:

12. That they all might be damned who believed not the
truth, but had pleasure in unrighteousness. (2 Thess.
2:10–12)

2. Preach the word; be instant in season, out of season;
reprove, rebuke, exhort with all longsuffering and
doctrine.

3. For the time will come when they will not endure
sound doctrine; but after their own lusts shall they
heap to themselves teachers, having itching ears;

4. And they shall turn away their ears from the truth,
and shall be turned unto fables. (2 Tim. 4:2–4)

If the people of Judah could have, they would have removed Micah and replaced him with a man walking in the spirit and lying and preaching of wine and strong drink. That is exactly what the church today is doing. The fact is that Micah would be chased out of most evangelical pulpits today!

THE PROPHET DEFENDED

In chapter 2:7, Micah answers an objection from the people and defends his own ministry. Micah's critics in Judah complain that he is misrepresenting God, that he is preaching a God of judgment, when God is a God of longsuffering mercy: "Is the spirit of the LORD straitened? are these his doings?"

The idea of "straitened" is shortened. A shortened spirit in scripture denotes impatience, anger, or even grief. Perhaps the closest to our text is Proverbs 14:29: "He that is slow to wrath is of great understanding: but he that is hasty of spirit exalteth folly." "Micah, are you saying that God is becoming impatient with us, the house of Jacob? Micah, that is impossible. God would never judge us!"

The idea that God could judge his own people was against their own deeply ingrained creed, a creed that dated back to Moses: "The LORD, the LORD God, merciful and gracious, long-suffering, and abundant in goodness and truth, keeping mercy for thousands, forgiving iniquity and transgression and sin" (Ex. 34:6–7). The idea that God could be angry with Judah, so angry that he would disinherit them and send them into Babylon, was preposterous, if not blasphemous. Is the longsuffering God suddenly exasperated with Judah?

Judah was convinced that Micah must be wrong. The acts that Micah described simply could not be the doings of Jehovah.

We encounter the same objections in the church today: God

is too loving to send judgment; I could never believe in a God who would punish people. Whenever there is a disaster, the cry goes out: "Is the Spirit of the Lord straitened? Are these his doings?" "No," the answer is given, "they are the devil's doings." The tragedy is that the people denied that God would send judgment right up to the day and hour when Jerusalem finally fell. The false church will deny the judgment of God right up to the day and hour of Christ's return.

The answer of Micah to this objection is twofold. First, God's mercy is shown to the house of Jacob, but not to that which simply calls itself the house of Jacob. Second, God's goodness is shown to those who walk uprightly, not to the wicked.

Notice Micah's sharp words in chapter 2:7: "O thou that art named the house of Jacob." Micah addresses the whole nation, and the whole nation is named the house of Jacob, but not every person in Israel, Judah, and Jerusalem is a child of God. The majority of the nation is the reprobate shell, but the promises of salvation pertain only to the elect kernel, the true Israel. The whole nation hears the threats and the promises.

"Do not my words do good to him that walketh uprightly?" (v. 7). To walk uprightly means to frame one's life according to God's commands and to live in harmony with God's law. But the people were not walking uprightly. They were walking perversely and crookedly. Therefore, Micah could only preach judgment to them in the hope that some of them would turn to God in true repentance. Then God's word would do good to those who walk uprightly.

We find the way of escape in the cross of Christ. That is where the longsuffering of God and the judgment of God are revealed. Jesus Christ is the only one who really walked uprightly, whose entire life was in harmony with all of God's commandments. Therefore, you would expect that God's word would do good to him. You would expect that God would richly bless him for his obedient, upright walk. You would expect God to spare his own Son who loved and obeyed him. But if God had spared his own Son, he could not have spared us. We have not walked uprightly. Therefore, God sent Jesus Christ, the upright mediator, to represent a guilty, crooked, and perverse people. Because Jesus Christ represented us, he suffered the judgment, curse, and wrath of God against our sins. Our crookedness and perverseness were accounted his, and his righteousness and uprightness were accounted ours. He received judgment, and we received mercy. Out of deep gratitude to him, we do walk uprightly and we do hear his word, a word that to us is not an annoying dropping but a refreshing shower of blessings.

Chapter 5

The Coming
of the Breaker

12. I will surely assemble, O Jacob, all of thee; I will surely
    gather the remnant of Israel; I will put them together
    as the sheep of Bozrah, as the flock in the midst of
    their fold: they shall make great noise by reason of the
    multitude of men.
13. The breaker is come up before them: they have broken
    up, and have passed through the gate, and are gone
    out by it: and their king shall pass before them, and
    the Lord on the head of them. (Micah 2:12–13)

The prophets, like the book of Revelation in the New Testament, rarely specify time. We might find that unusual and
expect that the prophets would tell us when things will happen.
The closest that the prophets ever come to specifying time is with
expressions such as "in that day," "in the latter days," or "after
those things." In our text, there is no temporal indicator at all
except for the future tense: "I will…" Yet the text is describing a
distant future.

It is also common in the prophets to introduce an abrupt
change of subject. That is the case with the end of chapter 2:
Micah moves from judgment to salvation. He moves from the

judgment of the heathen reapportioning Israel's fields and Israel departing from the land, which is not her rest, to the gathering, multiplication, and redemption of the remnant.

John Calvin, who otherwise is an excellent commentator on the prophets, erred here. He could not believe a sudden change of subject was possible at this point. Therefore, he interpreted the text as a prophecy of further judgment. In Calvin's view, God threatens to gather Israel together to destroy her. His understanding of the passage is that God will bring the Breaker, Nebuchadnezzar and the Babylonians or Sennacherib and the Assyrians, to break down Jerusalem's wall and carry them away captive. He understands this as the humiliation that Judah suffered when she was carried away with Zedekiah, her last king, at the head of her. But most commentators disagree with Calvin. This text is a prophecy of salvation, not judgment.

The greatest proof for this interpretation is that the remnant of Israel usually refers to that which is saved, not to that which is destroyed:

> And I will make her that halted a remnant, and her that was cast far off a strong nation: and the LORD shall reign over them in mount Zion from henceforth, even for ever. (Mic. 4:7)

7. And the remnant of Jacob shall be in the midst of many people as a dew from the Lord, as the showers upon the grass, that tarrieth not for man, nor waiteth for the sons of men.
8. And the remnant of Jacob shall be among the Gentiles in the midst of many people as a lion among the beasts of the forest, as a young lion among the flocks of sheep: who, if he go through, both treadeth down, and teareth in pieces, and none can deliver. (5:7–8)

Who is a God like unto thee, that pardoneth iniquity, and passeth by the transgression of the remnant of his heritage? he retaineth not his anger for ever, because he delighteth in mercy. (7:18)

Besides that, if the Breaker were to lead the people from Jerusalem he would not come up but go down. In the Bible, one always goes up to Jerusalem, and one always goes down from Jerusalem. Micah here prophesies great salvation, a source of great joy.

9. Break forth into joy, sing together, ye waste places of Jerusalem: for the Lord hath comforted his people, he hath redeemed Jerusalem.
10. The Lord hath made bare his holy arm in the eyes of all the nations; and all the ends of the earth shall see the salvation of our God.
11. Depart ye, depart ye, go ye out from thence, touch no unclean thing: go ye out of the midst of her; be ye clean, that bear the vessels of the Lord.
12. For ye shall not go out with haste, nor go by flight: for the Lord will go before you; and the God of Israel will be your rearward. (Isa. 52:9–12)

Christ is the breaker, which means that our text is an important prophecy of salvation, one that we neglect but that is as important as, if less familiar than, Micah 5:2.

GATHERING JACOB

In Micah 2:12, God makes a beautiful promise: "I will surely assemble...I will surely gather." A gathering presupposes a prior scattering. Therefore, judgment is implied. We see that Micah's prophecy of hope does not contradict his previous prophecy of judgment. The false prophets, the ones prophesying of wine and strong drink (v. 11), flatly denied that God would scatter his people. But Micah, the true prophet, teaches that God will scatter the nation in the Assyrian and Babylonian captivities in order to gather them again.

In scripture, God scatters in judgment and he gathers in mercy: "For a small moment have I forsaken thee; but with great mercies will I gather thee. In a little wrath I hid my face from thee for a moment; but with everlasting kindness will I have mercy on thee, saith the LORD thy Redeemer" (Isa. 54:7–8). "In that day, saith the LORD, will I assemble her that halteth, and I will gather her that is driven out, and her that I have afflicted" (Mic. 4:6).

God scatters the entire nation in judgment, the nation he calls "O thou that art named the house of Jacob" in chapter 2:7. The purpose of such a terrible scattering is to refine his people: they are like wheat to be harvested, but in order for the wheat to be gathered, the chaff and husks have to be scattered. Only after the "Israel in name only" have been winnowed out of Israel will God gather again the real Israel, whom he calls "O Jacob" and "the remnant of Israel" in verse 12. The announcement of a future gathering comes in the form of a promise, which is a sure and certain word, designed to comfort and assure the people of God in the nation.

The Hebrew is emphatic in the form of a promise. Literally, Micah writes, "Assembling I shall assemble," and, "Gathering I shall gather." That is how one writes with emphasis and makes a promise in Hebrew. The technical grammatical term is infinitive absolute. Thus the KJV rightly translates it as "I will surely." This was necessary because the promise of a future restoration seemed impossible, and from Israel's perspective it was impossible. God wants his people to have assurance, so he inspires his prophet to use this grammatical construction, which he expresses in the perfect tense: "The breaker *is come up*" (v. 13, emphasis added).

To whom is the promise addressed? Not to Israel as a nation, not to all Israel head for head, but to the whole remnant of Israel. "I will surely assemble, O Jacob, all of thee; I will surely gather the remnant of Israel" (v. 12). Not one of the elect remnant of Israel will be lost. That is God's promise here. Yes, they will be scattered; yes, they will be tempted to despair; but God's promise is sure.

But "Jacob" or "the remnant of Israel" does not refer to the elect only among the Jews. If it did, there would be no gospel for us. We are the seed of Abraham, part of God's Israel:

> 24. Even us, whom he hath called, not of the Jews only, but also of the Gentiles?
> 25. As he saith also in Osee, I will call them my people, which were not my people; and her beloved, which was not beloved. (Rom. 9:24–25)

> And if ye be Christ's, then are ye Abraham's seed, and heirs according to the promise. (Gal. 3:29)

> 10. For this is the covenant that I will make with the house of Israel after those days, saith the Lord; I will put my laws into their mind, and write them in their hearts: and I will be to them a God, and they shall be to me a people:
> 11. And they shall not teach every man his neighbour, and every man his brother, saying, Know the Lord: for all shall know me, from the least to the greatest.
> 12. For I will be merciful to their unrighteousness, and their sins and their iniquities will I remember no more. (Heb. 8:10–12)

In the New Testament, the gathering of Jacob is not confined to the gathering of one nation, and therefore the fulfillment of this prophecy goes beyond the return from Babylon. The gathering of the people of God is spiritual.

When Israel returned after seventy years in captivity, as a remnant of a remnant, that return constituted but a dim shadow of the gathering promised here. At her beginning, especially under David and Solomon, Israel had consisted of twelve tribes. But ten tribes were lost in Assyria, leaving only Judah and Benjamin. Of those two tribes, only a small remnant returned: a remnant of a remnant. As wonderful and miraculous as the return from Babylon was, it served a greater future gathering in Jesus Christ.

The gathering occurs when men, women, and children (from whatever nation) are called by the Holy Spirit through the preaching of the gospel into fellowship with God in Christ. The work of Jesus Christ the Savior is described as a gathering: "Other sheep I have, which are not of this fold: them also I must bring, and they shall hear my voice; and there shall be one fold, and one shepherd" (John 10:16). "Not for that nation only, but that also he should gather together in one the children of God that were scattered abroad" (11:52).

We who have heard and believed the message of the gospel have been gathered. It is the will and purpose as well as the promise of God to gather all his elect. Notice that the work of gathering is God's ("*I* will surely"). We do not gather the church. We are simply used as instruments in that great work.

The gathering here is described in terms of a shepherd gathering his sheep, a very common biblical figure. As God's sheep, we are a particular kind of animal. The Bible uses the figure of sheep to teach us how weak and helpless we are. The Bible uses the figure of sheep to teach us how stubborn, foolish, and wayward we are. The Bible teaches us that Jehovah is our shepherd so that we might trust him in his love, faithfulness, strength, and care. Notice the language of sheep in the text: "I will put them together as the sheep of Bozrah, as the flock in the midst of their fold" (Mic. 2:12).

Jehovah, the God of Israel, the God who is faithful to his covenantal promises in Christ, will surely seek, find, gather, and protect all of his sheep and lambs. Be of good cheer, O Jacob, you will not languish in Babylon forever; and be of good cheer, beloved Christians, you will not perish in the misery of this world of sin and death. Jehovah will gather you and your children unto himself.

MULTIPLYING THE REMNANT

God promises to multiply the remnant. A multiplying presupposes a diminishing. Again, the fact that there will be only a remnant perfectly harmonizes with Micah's prophecy of judgment. Micah teaches here that Israel and Judah will be so judged, so decimated, that only a remnant will be left to enjoy the future promised salvation.

A remnant simply means the leftovers of something. If an army goes to war, and most of the soldiers die but a few return in defeat, they are the remnant. If a nation is slaughtered, but only a few survive, they are the remnant. Elsewhere, Isaiah the prophet speaks of the remnant: "Except the LORD of hosts had left unto us a very small remnant, we should have been as Sodom, and we should have been like unto Gomorrah" (Isa. 1:9).

Oh yes, God will have mercy on Jacob and on Israel, but only on a small remnant of them. The Assyrians and the Babylonians will storm into the land, destroy the cities and villages, slaughter men, women, and children, and carry the rest away into captivity.

The land of Canaan will be inhabited by a foreign power, and indeed after the return from captivity the land will never belong to the Jews again. But through it all, a remnant, a very small remnant, will be preserved.

Almost paradoxically the prophet Micah speaks of a multiplying of the remnant. A remnant is, almost by definition, small, but this remnant will be a multitude of men (Mic. 2:12).

Again, Micah employs the sheep metaphor to depict this. He calls the returning gathered remnant "the sheep of Bozrah" (v. 12). Bozrah was the capital of Edom, the nation of Esau. The name *Bozrah* means "sheepfold." Bozrah was known for its shepherding. To be like the sheep of Bozrah means to be a great multitude of sheep.

Moreover, Micah promises that the remnant Jehovah gathers "shall make great noise by reason of the multitude of men" (v. 12). Micah uses onomatopoeia (a word that sounds like the word it describes: "They shall hum with men." The verb *make a great noise* can be positive or negative, depending on the context. The figure is very graphic: go to a farm where animals are crammed into a narrow pen and listen to the sounds of the sheep, and you will get an idea of Micah's meaning here. A sheep pen filled to bursting with the hustle and bustle, hum and buzz of animals in an overcrowded flock—that is the idea of the multiplication of the remnant.

The fulfillment of this prophecy can hardly be confined to the days when a remnant returned to Jerusalem from Babylon. According to Ezra 2:64, only 42,360 returned under Zerubbabel and Joshua.

It may come as a surprise to many Christians, but when the prophets promise an overcrowding in Israel, they teach the gathering of the Gentiles. That is how God promises to multiply the remnant of Israel. If God confined the gathering and multiplying of his people to one nation, there would not be a fulfillment of this beautiful prophecy. When God gathers into his church all the nations, the sheep pen is filled to bursting. That was what Jesus promised to do in John 10:16: "And other sheep I have which are not of this fold: them also I must bring, and they shall hear my voice; and there shall be one fold, and one shepherd."

The New Testament makes abundantly clear that not only does God have one people, the church, but also that the church is the fulfillment of the Old Testament. This is in opposition to the view of dispensationalism, which teaches that the gathering of the Gentiles into one people was never revealed in the Old Testament. In fact, dispensationalism teaches that God's gathering of the Gentiles into the church is a secondary plan, a parenthesis. Later, they contend, after God has finished with the Gentiles, he will return to gather the Jews. But the Bible teaches that God gathers Jews and Gentiles into the church. There is no "later" after the gathering of the church.

Let us prove this from the Old Testament prophets:

18. Lift up thine eyes round about, and behold: all these gather themselves together, and come to thee. As I live, saith the Lord, thou shalt surely clothe thee with them all, as with an ornament, and bind them on thee, as a bride doeth.

19. For thy waste and thy desolate places, and the land of thy destruction, shall even now be too narrow by reason of the inhabitants, and they that swallowed thee up shall be far away.

20. The children which thou shalt have, after thou hast lost the other, shall say again in thine ears, The place is too strait for me: give place to me that I may dwell.

21. Then shalt thou say in thine heart, Who hath begotten me these, seeing I have lost my children, and am desolate, a captive, and removing to and fro? and who

hath brought up these? Behold, I was left alone; these, where had they been?

22. Thus saith the Lord God, Behold, I will lift up mine hand to the Gentiles, and set up my standard to the people: and they shall bring thy sons in their arms, and thy daughters shall be carried upon their shoulders.

23. And kings shall be thy nursing fathers, and their queens thy nursing mothers: they shall bow down to thee with their face toward the earth, and lick up the dust of thy feet; and thou shalt know that I am the Lord: for they shall not be ashamed that wait for me. (Isa. 49:18–23)

1. Sing, O barren, thou that didst not bear; break forth into singing, and cry aloud, thou that didst not travail with child: for more are the children of the desolate than the children of the married wife, saith the Lord.

2. Enlarge the place of thy tent, and let them stretch forth the curtains of thine habitations: spare not, lengthen thy cords, and strengthen thy stakes;

3. For thou shalt break forth on the right hand and on the left; and thy seed shall inherit the Gentiles, and make the desolate cities to be inhabited. (54:1–3)

1. But in the last days it shall come to pass, that the mountain of the house of the Lord shall be established in the top of the mountains, and it shall be exalted above the hills; and people shall flow unto it.

2. And many nations shall come, and say, Come, and let us go up to the mountain of the Lord, and to the house of the God of Jacob; and he will teach us of his ways, and we will walk in his paths: for the law shall go forth of Zion, and the word of the Lord from Jerusalem. (Mic. 4:1–2)

Again we notice that all of this is the work of God: "*I* will put them together" (2:12, emphasis added). We do not make the one church of Jew and Gentile. That is the wonderwork of God in Jesus Christ:

19. Now therefore ye are no more strangers and foreigners, but fellow-citizens with the saints, and of the household of God;
20. And are built upon the foundation of the apostles and prophets, Jesus Christ himself being the chief corner stone;
21. In whom all the building fitly framed together groweth unto an holy temple in the Lord:
22. In whom ye also are builded together for an habitation of God through the Spirit. (Eph. 2:19–22)

BREAKING THROUGH THE GATE

God promises to deliver his people from confinement. Look at the beautiful imagery. God gathers his sheep; then he multiplies them so that they are bursting through overcrowding; and finally he breaks down the gate and delivers them into freedom.

To break up and pass through the gate (Mic. 2:13) presupposes some kind of imprisonment. The imprisonment envisaged here is first the Babylonian captivity. The gate of verse 13 is most likely the gate of Babylon, through which Israel exited the Babylonian captivity after seventy years.

The gate really refers to any obstacle or barrier that prevents the freedom of God's people. The figure is of a thick gate behind which God's people are trapped with nowhere to go as they huddle as a frightened flock of sheep. The gate, therefore, has a spiritual application: it is the gate of salvation through which we must pass to be delivered from our sins. "Open to me the gates of righteousness: I will go into them, and I will praise the LORD: this gate of the LORD, into which the righteous shall enter" (Ps. 118:19–20). "I will go before thee, and make the crooked places straight: I will break in pieces the gates of brass, and cut in sunder the bars of iron" (Isa. 45:2).

For us there are the gates of hell, thick gates that we can by no means overcome. They are the gates of the kingdom of darkness in which we are trapped. Our sins, death, the grave, the devil, the curse, and hell must be overcome for us to be saved, but we are utterly powerless to overcome such obstacles and barriers to our salvation. What will become of this greatly multiplied flock of sheep huddled behind the gates of Babylon and confined behind the gates of the kingdom of darkness?

Into this hopeless situation comes the Breaker of Micah 2:13. Who is he and what does he do?

The Breaker is the one who breaks down the wall and brings us through the gate. The word *break* has several meanings, but the main idea is of great force and violence. For example, God might break forth in judgment against someone (as he did with Uzzah in 2 Samuel 6:8). David breaks through the defenses of an enemy in 2 Samuel 5:20, a victory David attributes to God and calls the place "The LORD breaks through." Or the word means to make a breach or a hole in a wall (2 Kings 14:13).

This breaker is none other than Jesus Christ himself. He is called "their king," and he is even called "the LORD" who leads his remnant forth at the head of them (Mic. 2:13). Jehovah, in the person of his Son Jesus Christ, breaks down the gate and leads his gathered and multiplied remnant into salvation and fellowship. Perhaps we could translate the term as "Jehovah the Smasher," or even "Jehovah the Bulldozer" or "Jehovah the Battering Ram."

The idea is that Jesus Christ is no weakling, no ineffectual savior. He breaks down whatever holds his people back and brings them into freedom. He leaves none of them behind: "I will surely assemble, O Jacob, all of thee…they shall make great noise…The breaker is come up" (vv. 12–13).

What a glorious prophecy of Christ! Jesus Christ is the breaker, the king who leads his people because he went ahead of them and died for them on the cross.

How does Jesus Christ bash down, smash down, or break through the gates of hell? There is only one way in which he could do that. He had to disarm those gates. The power of death (or the sting of death) is sin. Jesus had to remove the power and sting of death, and that meant removing sin. But Jesus could remove sin in only one way: by becoming responsible for our sins and paying the penalty. Once Jesus had paid the penalty, the power and sting of death were removed.

How could Jesus bash down, smash, or break the devil? How could he crush that old serpent's head? The power of the devil is sin also, for it is because of sin that the devil has a right to rule over us and enslave us. Therefore, Jesus had to deliver us from the grasp of the devil by paying a ransom price to the justice of God, and he did that, as we know, on the cross (Col. 2:14–15).

In Micah's day, these truths were dimly seen. However, they were depicted to God's saints in the animal sacrifices in the temple.

Having bashed, smashed, and broken through sin, the grave, the devil, the curse, death, and hell, Jesus rose again from the dead. That was the coming back to life again of the Breaker. That is how he now leads us out through that great gaping hole that he has left in the gates of hell.

Does that not fill you with confidence? Your Savior is the Breaker! He is our shepherd, our savior, our king, and our Breaker.

Chapter 6

Judgment Corrupted by Zion's Butchers

1. And I said, Hear, I pray you, O heads of Jacob, and ye princes of the house of Israel; Is it not for you to know judgment?
2. Who hate the good, and love the evil; who pluck off their skin from off them, and their flesh from off their bones;
3. Who also eat the flesh of my people, and flay their skin from off them; and they break their bones, and chop them in pieces, as for the pot, and as flesh within the caldron.
4. Then shall they cry unto the Lord, but he will not hear them: he will even hide his face from them at that time, as they have behaved themselves ill in their doings...

9. Hear this, I pray you, ye heads of the house of Jacob, and princes of the house of Israel, that abhor judgment, and pervert all equity.
10. They build up Zion with blood, and Jerusalem with iniquity.
11. The heads thereof judge for reward, and the priests thereof teach for hire, and the prophets thereof divine

for money: yet will they lean upon the Lord, and say, Is
not the Lord among us? none evil can come upon us.

12. Therefore shall Zion for your sake be plowed as a field,
and Jerusalem shall become heaps, and the mountain
of the house as the high places of the forest. (Micah
3:1–4, 9–12)

Chapter 3 gives us a snapshot of life in Jerusalem in c. 700
BC. The picture Micah paints for us is a very ugly and shocking
portrait. What he describes is the corruption occurring behind
the scenes. He rips away the religious mask to reveal the ugly
truth. Micah spares none, especially not the rich and powerful.

We have seen this already in the prophecy of Micah. In chapter
1, Micah spoke of unspecified sin. In chapter 2, Micah probed the
bedrooms of the rich landowners as they plotted to steal and then
stole the inheritance of their fellow Israelites. Only the coming of
the Breaker described at the end of chapter 2 will bring salvation.

But Micah has given us only a brief glimpse of the future prom-
ised in Christ. We have longed for him, as the elect remnant in
Judah have done. Nevertheless, chapter 3 brings us abruptly back to
Micah's present, because Micah has not finished exposing sin.

There is corruption not only in real estate and property, but also
in the courts. What is the oppressed Israelite to do if he has been
wronged by his neighbor? Under the law he could go to the judges
and ask for justice, but the judges had become butchers and cannibals. Instead of helping the people, they devoured them and spat out
the bones. Remember that this is a description of sin *in the church*.

JUDGMENT REQUIRED

Judgment in the Old Testament is much more than punishment
for sin. To receive judgment means to receive what is right under
the law. Judgment is a key idea in Micah 3:

1. And I said, Hear, I pray you, O heads of Jacob, and ye princes of the house of Israel; Is it not for you to know *judgment*? (emphasis added)

8. But truly I am full of power by the spirit of the Lord, and of *judgment*, and of might, to declare unto Jacob his transgression, and to Israel his sin. (emphasis added)

9. Hear this, I pray you, ye heads of the house of Jacob, and princes of the house of Israel, that abhor *judgment*, and pervert all *equity*. (emphasis added)

11. The heads thereof *judge* for reward, and the priests thereof teach for hire, and the prophets thereof divine for money: yet will they lean upon the Lord, and say, Is not the Lord among us? none evil can come upon us. (emphasis added)

So that Israel and Judah might be just societies under the law of God, Jehovah appointed various officers: heads, princes (vv. 1, 9), priests, and prophets (v. 11). These officers were appointed at various times in Israel's history. Moses first appointed them in Exodus 18:21–23:

21. Moreover thou shalt provide out of all the people able men, such as fear God, men of truth, hating covetousness; and place such over them, to be rulers of thousands, and rulers of hundreds, rulers of fifties, and rulers of tens:

22. And let them judge the people at all seasons: and it shall be, that every great matter they shall bring unto thee, but every small matter they shall judge: so shall it be easier for thyself, and they shall bear the burden with thee.

23. If thou shalt do this thing, and God command thee so, then thou shalt be able to endure, and all this people shall also go to their place in peace.

The law of Moses later legislated for such men in Deuteronomy 16:18–20:

18. Judges and officers shalt thou make thee in all thy gates, which the Lord thy God giveth thee, throughout thy tribes: and they shall judge the people with just judgment.
19. Thou shalt not wrest judgment; thou shalt not respect persons, neither take a gift: for a gift doth blind the eyes of the wise, and pervert the words of the righteous.
20. That which is altogether just shalt thou follow, that thou mayest live, and inherit the land which the Lord thy God giveth thee.

Good kings such as Jehoshaphat appointed judges:

4. And Jehoshaphat dwelt at Jerusalem: and he went out again through the people from Beersheba to mount Ephraim, and brought them back unto the Lord God of their fathers.
5. And he set judges in the land throughout all the fenced cities of Judah, city by city,
6. And said to the judges, Take heed what ye do: for ye judge not for man, but for the Lord, who is with you in the judgment.
7. Wherefore now let the fear of the Lord be upon you; take heed and do it: for there is no iniquity with the Lord our God, nor respect of persons, nor taking of gifts.

8. Moreover in Jerusalem did Jehoshaphat set of the Levites, and of the priests, and of the chief of the fathers of Israel, for the judgment of the Lord, and for controversies, when they returned to Jerusalem.

9. And he charged them, saying, Thus shall ye do in the fear of the Lord, faithfully, and with a perfect heart.

10. And what cause soever shall come to you of your brethren that dwell in their cities, between blood and blood, between law and commandment, statutes and judgments, ye shall even warn them that they trespass not against the Lord, and so wrath come upon you, and upon your brethren: this do, and ye shall not trespass. (2 Chron. 19:4–10)

Since we know that Israel or Judah is the Old Testament church, we apply this word of God not to civil authorities, but to the officebearers of the New Testament church. Micah's concern is for judgment in Israel, Judah, Jerusalem, and Zion; and our concern is for judgment in the consistory room, the diaconate, the classis and synod, and the pulpit. That is the judgment that is corrupted in today's church. About corruption in society we say as Paul, "For what have I to do to judge them also that are without? do not ye judge them that are within? But them that are without God judgeth" (1 Cor. 5:12–13).

Micah confronts the leaders of his day with their calling and their dereliction of duty: "Is it not for you to know judgment?" (Mic. 3:1). This is a rhetorical question, which has more impact than a simple statement. Of course it is for the leaders of Judah to know judgment!

To know judgment means, first, to have a thorough acquaintance with the law of God, which is the basis, in the Old Testament, of all true judgment. But knowledge is the bare minimum: the judges must also love judgment, delight in judgment, be wise to apply judgment, and be scrupulously honest in their administration of judgment. The judges must do this out of a love for God, the lawgiver, and out of a love for their neighbor whose rights, privileges, and responsibilities under the law they are called to safeguard.

This applies to the officebearers of the New Testament church, and this word of God should be written above every ecclesiastical assembly: "Is it not for you to know judgment?" When the consistory decides a case or when a broader assembly deliberates a motion, the aim must be to know, love, and administer judgment. The goal of all decisions must be the glory of God, the welfare of the church, and the good of the neighbor. Corruption and dishonesty must not be so much as named among us. This is all the more serious because the judges of Micah's day and the officebearers of our day are administering judgment among God's people (v. 3) and building Zion and Jerusalem (v. 10).

Judgment, as we said, is to receive what is right under the law. Therefore, judgment takes two forms.

First, there are positive judgments. Judgment required that an innocent person was acquitted, a good and virtuous person was rewarded, a vulnerable person was protected, an aggrieved or victimized person was avenged, and a person from whom property was stolen had his property restored to him.

The Old Testament law had very detailed and precise requirements of justice.

For example, if a farmer complained that a neighbor stole his sheep, the judge must examine the case, and the farmer must have his sheep restored fourfold. If a widow complained that a neighbor had treated her cruelly, the judge must punish the widow's enemy and restore her rights to her. That was positive judgment: a person received what was his right under the law, and it was the judge's calling to protect the people's rights.

This is true in the New Testament as well. The officebearers of the church must uphold and protect the truth and decide in favor of the innocent and right, no matter what social status or position the complainant has. The officebearers must insist that the truth is faithfully preached. They may not tolerate false doctrine because it is popular or because a popular preacher is promoting it. The officebearers must legislate in such a way that God's commandments are kept. They must not make unjust laws or refuse to enforce God's law.

Second, there are negative judgments. Judgment required that a guilty person be condemned and punished. This was the requirement, for example, in Deuteronomy 25:1: "If there be a controversy between men, and they come unto judgment, that the judges may judge them; then they shall justify the righteous, and condemn the wicked." This was necessary because if the wicked are not punished, sin spreads and corrupts the nation, or the church. The temptation, of course, was to let the wicked go free because of their position in society or in the church. Judgment must be blind and not a respecter of persons.

The same is true regarding the work of the church of the New Testament. In order to build Zion and Jerusalem and to build up the church, there must be fair, equitable church discipline. The elders must not refuse to discipline a member because he is rich, powerful, related to an officebearer, or for some other carnal reason. In short, judgment must be in harmony with the law; it must be equity (Mic. 3:9).

JUDGMENT DENIED

Nevertheless, the judges, rulers, princes, priests, and prophets in Micah's day did not know judgment. Micah's description of the moral character of Judah's judges is unsparing.

First, they hated judgment. In verse 9, Micah uses the word *abhor*. To abhor is to view with extreme disgust and loathing, to detest, and to seek to rid oneself of the hated thing. They hated the right ways of God's law, and therefore, by implication, they hated God himself who had given the law to govern the life of the people. They hated acquitting the innocent; they hated rewarding the good; they hated protecting the vulnerable; they hated vindicating and avenging the wronged; they hated restoring the rights of the victimized; they hated showing mercy to the oppressed; and they hated punishing the guilty.

Therefore, says Micah in verse 2, they hated the good: they hated good people, good actions, and goodness itself. They hated righteousness, holiness, justice, and equity; and they hated kindness, benevolence, and mercy. How awful! That is a description of the officebearers of the church!

Second, they perverted all equity (v. 9). To pervert is to twist. Hatred is the attitude, and perversion is the activity that flows from the attitude. Whatever the right and just outcome in harmony with the law might be, they twisted it. By their wickedness they made sure that the innocent suffered and were robbed of their rights and privileges, and that the wicked prospered. Thus the thief, the oppressor, or the murderer would escape unpunished because he was able to bribe the judges.

This is because they loved the evil (v. 2): whatever was morally corrupt, a vice or a sin, any form of exploitation or injustice they loved. They had a deep affection for and delight in whatever caused harm to the cause of righteousness and whatever hurt their neighbor. You can be sure that they denied these charges vehemently, but the prophet Micah exposed them for what they truly were.

Third, and most striking, they were cruel. The judges who were called by God to shepherd the people and to guide them in righteousness and love had become butchers and cannibals. Micah paints in bold colors a shockingly gruesome portrait of these men. He does this by lingering on the details and describing step by step how cruel and callous these men were.

First, they skin the people alive: "pluck off…flay" (vv. 2–3). Second, they tear off the people's flesh: "pluck off…their flesh from off their bones" (v. 2). Third, they eat the flesh, devouring it with the blood still in it, so greedy and voracious is their appetite: "who also eat the flesh of my people" (v. 3). Fourth, they break their bones (v. 3). Fifth, they smash the carcass to pieces so that it can be rammed into a pot or cauldron, and finally they cook whatever is left over (v. 3). Shockingly and shamefully, the victims of their cannibalism are *God's own people*.

All of this Micah calls "build[ing] up Zion with blood, and Jerusalem with iniquity" (v. 10).

Micah explains what he means by this cannibalistic butchering of the people in verse 11: oppression of the people through covetousness and the receiving of bribes. Remember, receiving of bribes was strictly forbidden in the law.

Picture the poor widow from chapter 2:9. She comes to seek justice at the local court, and surely her case is a clear one. She has been robbed of her home and she and her children cast out into the street. But instead of helping her, the judges decide against her and award all her property to the greedy landowner who oppressed her. Then the judges and the greedy landowners share the proceeds of the sale of the widow's house. The widow is figuratively skinned alive, her flesh torn from her bones and devoured, and her carcass cooked in the cauldron! That is how Micah explains the daily proceedings at the circuit court of Jerusalem!

The whole procedure is a perversion of equity, but there is nothing the widow can do except cry out to God for vengeance.

The whole legal system is rigged and everyone knows it, but no one will do anything about it, not even the prophets, as we shall see in the next chapter.

Sadly, such wickedness occurs in the church today. What Micah describes is relevant to us.

The cannibalistic butchers of our day are corrupt office-bearers, especially wicked pastors and teachers. In the New Testament, wolves are not corrupt politicians, judges, or others in the social sphere. (Of course, such men and women exist in the New Testament age, but they are not the focus of the prophets). The application of this word of God is not the corruption in Washington or Whitehall, but the corruption of the consistory, seminary, or broader assemblies of the church:

> Beware of false prophets, which come to you in sheep's clothing, but inwardly they are ravening wolves. (Matt. 7:15)

> For I know this, that after my departing shall grievous wolves enter in among you, not sparing the flock. (Acts 20:29)

> 2. Son of man, prophesy against the shepherds of Israel, prophesy, and say unto them, Thus saith the Lord God unto the shepherds; Woe be to the shepherds of Israel that do feed themselves! should not the shepherds feed the flocks?
> 3. Ye eat the fat, and ye clothe you with the wool, ye kill them that are fed: but ye feed not the flock. (Ezek. 34:2–3)

Pastors become butchers when they preach false doctrine especially out of covetousness and for their own personal gain. Pastors have, from their elevated position in the church, the potential for much cruelty and oppression of God's people. By preaching false doctrine while claiming the authority of God, they oppress people's consciences, holding them in bondage with threats of damnation or with a loss of blessing. They burden the people's consciences, forcing them to do and believe what is contrary to the word of God.

Then there is the heavy-handed authoritarianism of church leaders. When an officebearer in the New Testament church is guilty of treating certain members better because of their social position, and especially when he oppresses the poor in the congregation in the preaching, discipline, or diaconal work, he becomes a Micah 3 butcher:

1. My brethren, have not the faith of our Lord Jesus Christ, the Lord of glory, with respect of persons.
2. For if there come unto your assembly a man with a gold ring, in goodly apparel, and there come in also a poor man in vile raiment;
3. And ye have respect to him that weareth the gay clothing, and say unto him, Sit thou here in a good place; and say to the poor, Stand thou there, or sit here under my footstool:
4. Are ye not then partial in yourselves, and are become judges of evil thoughts? (James 2:1–4)

When an officebearer fleeces the people by demanding large offerings that the people cannot afford and threatens them if they question his ministry or demands, he becomes a Micah 3 butcher. When an ordinary believer becomes a tyrant in his family, as a husband and father, he becomes a Micah 3 butcher. This warning is very real, and the temptation to become a butcher is very strong.

The great sin that Micah describes in chapter 3 is hypocrisy or hiding behind a religious profession to justify one's sin. It ought to be very humbling to us to discover that Zion's butchers were upstanding church members who trusted that God was blessing them.

Verse 11 says that they leaned upon the Lord, which is an expression that means faith or trust in Jehovah. These men were leaning upon God *to support their own wickedness*. Theirs was a hypocritical leaning upon God. The judges, after they devoured widows' houses, worshiped in the temple and pretended to be and claimed to be honest, religious men: "Woe unto you, scribes and Pharisees, hypocrites! for ye devour widows' houses, and for a pretence make long prayer: therefore ye shall receive the greater damnation" (Matt. 23:14). Modern Christians, after they have cruelly oppressed their wives and children, cheated their customers, or perpetrated injustice in the church courts, sit down in church and worship as if nothing had happened.

Micah 3:11 indicates that the wicked men of Judah boasted that Jehovah was among them and therefore no evil could come upon them. Did they not have the ordinances of God's worship: circumcision, sacrifices, the feast days, even preaching; and do we not have preaching and the sacraments? Was the temple not standing in their midst? Do we not have the worship of God in our midst? Were they not prospering? Were they not growing in numbers, power, and wealth? Was that not a sign of God's blessing? What did it matter that they had gained their riches by dishonest means? Were they not building Zion, and are we not building the church? Therefore, they concluded that, whatever Micah might say, no evil could come upon them, and no judgment could fall upon Jerusalem, God's city, and God's temple. They were immune from any form of divine retribution.

That is exactly the attitude of hypocrites in the church: God would never punish *me*. No matter how I live, no matter what I do, I am under God's blessing, exempt from judgment and also exempt from the obligation to live righteously by loving God and my neighbor.

JUDGMENT ANTICIPATED

Micah warns of a twofold judgment: one upon the nation and one upon the butchers themselves.

Zion shall "for your sake be plowed as a field" (Mic. 3:12). Zion's builders are her destroyers, because no one can build God's city with blood or iniquity. Jerusalem, Zion, and the church must be built in righteousness, and this Jerusalem's leaders refuse to do.

The judgment upon Jerusalem will be devastating. The city will suffer utter destruction so that the city along with its temple is wiped off the face of the earth. Jerusalem will have the same miserable end as did Samaria (1:6): the idea is that the land will be fit only for sowing crops and will be left in that state for so long that forests will grow there.

That is God's judgment upon every church and congregation that seeks to build the kingdom of God with blood and iniquity. Christ will, to use New Testament language, take away the golden candlestick and no longer dwell there by his word and Holy Spirit. It will happen, says Micah to the corrupt officebearers, "for your sake," that is, on account of you.

In addition, God will send a personal judgment: God will reject the cries of Zion's butchers (v. 4). They would not hear the cries of the oppressed people of God. Therefore, God will not hear them in the day of their calamity.

When the Babylonians come to level Jerusalem to the ground, Jehovah will not listen. When death comes to take these cruel, unjust men, there will be no salvation. And on the last day of judgment, when they cry, "Lord, Lord, have we not …?" God will not answer them, except with these chilling words: "Depart from me, ye that work iniquity" (Matt. 7:22–23).

This judgment was necessary to make way for the true office-bearer, even Jesus Christ. Micah in the earlier part of the book is preparing us for Christ in chapter 5:2. Only Christ can build Zion, not with blood, but with true and lasting judgment. The judgment and righteousness of the Messiah is a common biblical theme.

6. Thy throne, O God, is for ever and ever: the sceptre of thy kingdom is a right sceptre.
7. Thou lovest righteousness, and hatest wickedness: therefore God, thy God, hath anointed thee with the oil of gladness above thy fellows. (Ps. 45:6–7)

He shall judge thy people with righteousness, and thy poor with judgment. (72:2)

Of the increase of his government and peace there shall be no end, upon the throne of David, and upon his kingdom, to order it, and to establish it with judgment and with justice from henceforth even for ever. The zeal of the LORD of hosts will perform this (Isa. 9:7).

1. Behold my servant, whom I uphold; mine elect, in whom my soul delighteth; I have put my spirit upon him: he shall bring forth judgment to the Gentiles.
2. He shall not cry, nor lift up, nor cause his voice to be heard in the street.
3. A bruised reed shall he not break, and the smoking flax shall he not quench: he shall bring forth judgment unto truth.
4. He shall not fail nor be discouraged, till he have set judgment in the earth: and the isles shall wait for his law. (42:1–4)

Christ is not only the builder of the church, but the chief cornerstone:

5. Ye also, as lively stones, are built up a spiritual house, an holy priesthood, to offer up spiritual sacrifices, acceptable to God by Jesus Christ.
6. Wherefore also it is contained in the scripture, Behold, I lay in Sion a chief corner stone, elect, precious: and he that believeth on him shall not be confounded.
7. Unto you therefore which believe he is precious: but unto them which be disobedient, the stone which the builders disallowed, the same is made the head of the corner. (1 Pet. 2:5–7)

We find Christ in the text by way of contrast and anticipation. Christ knows and loves judgment. Christ exercises and fulfills the law. With Christ there is no respect of persons, no receiving of bribes, and no cruelty or oppression of his people.

As God's people suffered under Zion's butchers, they cried out for the Christ.

Christ performed judgment for his people by going to the cross, and there he bore the penalty of the law and earned for us the gift of righteousness. To his church, which he is still building, he gives godly officebearers through whom he feeds us with his word. Out of thankfulness to him, we live in judgment with our neighbor.

Chapter 7

Jehovah's Word against the Venal Prophets

5. Thus saith the Lord concerning the prophets that make my people err, that bite with their teeth, and cry, Peace; and he that putteth not into their mouths, they even prepare war against him.

6. Therefore night shall be unto you, that ye shall not have a vision; and it shall be dark unto you, that ye shall not divine; and the sun shall go down over the prophets, and the day shall be dark over them.

7. Then shall the seers be ashamed, and the diviners confounded: yea, they shall all cover their lips; for there is no answer of God.

8. But truly I am full of power by the spirit of the Lord, and of judgment, and of might, to declare unto Jacob his transgression, and to Israel his sin. (Micah 3:5–8)

In the last chapter, we saw corruption in Jerusalem in the days of Micah. God had given a law that explained how people were to live in mutual love. But the people (especially the leaders) hated the justice demanded in God's law. Instead, they loved injustice, exploitation, and greed.

Judah was like a rotten fish, rotten from the head down. It

was ruled by butchers instead of shepherds. Cannibals, who devoured God's people and spat out the bones, held high office in the land. The rich landowners and property developers cared nothing about the laws of inheritance, which ensured that a man could keep his property in Canaan. The judges cared nothing for the rights of the exploited.

We saw that this has a modern parallel in injustice in the church, especially in the ecclesiastical assemblies.

You might think that if there was one part of Judah and Jerusalem where there was still a love for truth and justice, it would be among those called to teach God's word. Should not the priests and prophets condemn such wicked living in their teaching and preaching on the sabbath day? Should there not be voices in the city crying out for obedience to God's law? As Malachi would say later: "For the priest's lips should keep knowledge, and they should seek the law at his mouth" (Mal. 2:7).

But even there, in the pulpits of the land, there was corruption. Instead of criticizing the wicked of the land, the prophets supported them. Instead of defending the righteous of the land, the prophets attacked them as a brood of vipers bite with their fangs. Thus Jerusalem in c. 700 BC was corrupt in all her parts, and Micah, as Jehovah's true prophet, was sent to preach to the prophets also.

THE VENAL PROPHETS

The word *venal* might be unfamiliar to many of us. It means "open to receiving bribes" or "able to be corrupted with money." That one word describes the prophets , and not only the prophets, for the judges, princes, heads, priests, and prophets were all venal.

The prophets in Micah's day were guilty of several serious sins. First, they were deceivers: "that make my people err" (Mic. 3:5).

The responsibility of a prophet is to preach the truth, the word of God. The prophet must tell the people what God says about certain kinds of behavior that displease him and must command the people to repent. The prophet must promise salvation and forgiveness of sins in the name of God to those who repent and believe. Equally, the prophet must threaten judgment upon the wicked, unbelieving, and impenitent. The prophet must do this without fear of what the audience will think, say, or do, no matter who the audience is, for Jehovah, whose word it is, is no respecter of persons.

But the prophets of Micah's day did not preach the truth. Instead, they preached lies, and they distorted the truth to suit themselves and their hearers. The verb *to make to err* means "to seduce or deceive." It was not a mistake or an accident that they did this. They knew the truth but deliberately lied for their own advantage. The verb also means "to cause to stagger like a drunkard." That is the effect of false doctrine upon a person. It makes him drunk so that spiritually he cannot live before the face of God.

To God's people, who needed to hear the comfort of salvation, the false prophets declared war. To the wicked, who needed to hear God's judgment, so that they might come to repentance and salvation or so that they might be left without excuse before God, the false prophets declared peace: "Because with lies ye have made the heart of the righteous sad, whom I have not made sad; and strengthened the hands of the wicked, that he should not return from his wicked way, by promising him life" (Ezek. 13:22).

Second, they were flatterers: "that bite with their teeth, and cry, Peace" (Mic. 3:5). They flattered the wicked by promising peace. They did this in contrast to Micah, who prophesied judgment. The Hebrew word for peace is *shalom*, which means much more than the absence of war. *Shalom* is wholeness or completeness. When a man has *shalom*, all is well with his soul, which means that all is well between his soul and God. One in *shalom* is reconciled to God and knows the blessing of God upon him.

God did not have a message of *shalom* for the wicked oppressors, butchers, and cannibals of Judah, and the false prophets had no right to preach that he did. God only has peace for his own people, his people who are sorry for their sins, who trust in him for salvation, and who live in obedience to him out of thankfulness. To God's people, the ones who needed to hear the word of peace, those who needed the comfort of the gospel, the false prophets declared war: "They even prepare war against him" (v. 5).

To summarize: the wicked in the land who cheated their neighbors heard a false message of peace (God will send prosperity; there is no judgment; Micah is just trying to scare you; he is misrepresenting our loving and merciful God; there is no need to repent). The true people of God, who suffered under the cruelty of the wicked, heard a false message of war.

Third, and really the reason for the first two sins, the false prophets were covetous: "he that putteth not into their mouths" (v. 5). The false prophets knew that their popularity and wealth depended on their bringing a message that would please the men who had the most money to give. If the false prophets, seeing the inheritance dispossessors of chapter 2, had condemned them for their cruelty and disregard for God's law, the rich landowners would not have paid them handsomely for their pleasing prophetic messages. If the false prophets, seeing the corrupt judges and rulers of chapter 3, had applied God's law to the situation and called the rulers to repentance, they could not have gotten their share of the money. In other words, if a man was willing to pay them, they would turn a blind eye to sin and deliver a prophecy of peace. As the saying goes, "He who pays the piper calls the tune."

But what of the poor, who either could not or would not give them a generous offering? "They even prepare war against him"

(v. 5). To them the false prophets were like serpents. The verb *bite* in verse 5 means the bite of a serpent or a snake. Their words were like the bite of a poisonous snake. If you wanted to receive a good word from Jehovah but had no money to give, they would "prepare war" against you, a "holy war" in the name of God.

Thus the corruption in Jerusalem was complete: it had infected the landowners, the businessmen, the courts, and even the pulpits of Judah! Venal prophets!

10. His watchmen are blind: they are all ignorant, they are all dumb dogs, they cannot bark; sleeping, lying down, loving to slumber.
11. Yea, they are greedy dogs which can never have enough, and they are shepherds that cannot understand: they all look to their own way, every one for his gain, from his quarter.
12. Come ye, say they, I will fetch wine, and we will fill ourselves with strong drink; and to-morrow shall be as this day, and much more abundant. (Isa. 56:10–12)

Micah's prophecy, written some 2,700 years ago, is as relevant today as it was then. We have today venal pastors, ministers, teachers, and theologians. Venal pastors and ministers accommodate their messages to what the people want to hear, not what they need to hear.

Peter speaks about such in the New Testament. Second Peter 2:1 teaches, "But there were false prophets also among the people, even as there shall be false teachers among you." Verse 2 adds, "And many shall follow their pernicious ways; by reason of whom the way of truth shall be evil spoken of." Verse 3 concludes, "And through covetousness shall they with feigned [pretended] words make merchandise of you: whose judgment now of a long time lingereth not, and their damnation slumbereth not."

This is always a grave temptation for any minister. When a pastor looks at his text and realizes what it means, sometimes he trembles and thinks, "Can I really preach *that*? If I preach that, will people leave, will people be offended, or will the young people leave?" That is the concern many pastors and churches have. Of course, no pastor wants people to leave, and he never seeks deliberately to offend. A pastor wants people to repent and believe and live as godly Christians.

But the word of God has an effect, and the venal pastor or teacher, like the venal prophet of Micah's day, does not want that effect. He wants to change the message to get the effect he wants. Thus he preaches peace to the wicked (especially the rich wicked, or to a large number of wicked people) and preaches war to the godly (especially the poor, powerless godly, whose numbers do not concern him).

The fundamental sin of the false teacher today is that he does not preach Christ; and the reason he does not preach Christ is that he does not preach sin and thus the need for Christ. A false teacher today preaches a top-heavy and false message about God's love, that God has a wonderful plan for everybody's life, and that God would never send judgment. God's love is a wonderful truth, but God's love cannot be promised to a group of ungodly, impenitent, unbelieving persons. They cannot hear about God's love until they understand their own sin.

When Micah's contemporaries were cheating their neighbors, the last thing they needed to hear was God's love from the false prophets. "You do not need to worry about God's judgment. God loves you anyway, and God has promised peace to you." The same is true today: an unbeliever cannot appreciate the gospel of forgiveness in Christ without knowing why Christ came, why Christ died, and why Christ rose again. That is why the false gospel will fill churches but will do no real spiritual good to the members of such churches. Micah's hearers believed in God. They worshiped in the temple, and they claimed to be true Israelites, but their lives told a different story.

That is true today too: a man might come to church, get excited about the worship and programs, but live in unbelief, cheat on his wife, and defraud his customers at his business. Or a person might come to church on Sunday but spend his Friday nights getting drunk and half the week viewing pornography on the Internet. When the minister is afraid to address such sins in the preaching, he just tells the congregation that God is love and that repentance is not necessary in the Christian life, and he does so to keep the people coming and the offerings flowing.

Christ came into the world to save sinners, but he came to save them in such a way that they are delivered from their sins and no longer live in their sins. When God's people hear that Jesus died for their sins, they are filled with wonder, with sorrow over their sins, and with gratitude for the salvation. But there will be no true repentance over sin unless sin is preached and Christ is preached as the savior of sinners, not as a helper or one to make your life easy, and certainly not as a facilitator or approver of sin. Therefore, easy believism, antinomianism, and moralistic preaching will never save anyone.

JEHOVAH'S COURAGEOUS MESSENGER

Into this situation of corruption in the business world, courts, and even pulpits, God sends Micah.

In chapter 3:8, Micah contrasts himself sharply with the false prophets and shows us what true ministry is. Micah makes a claim that no false, venal prophet ought to make: he brings Jehovah's word because he is filled with the Spirit. "Thus saith the LORD" (v. 5); "But truly I am full of power by the Spirit of the LORD" (v. 8).

To be filled with the Spirit does not mean what many today think it means. To be filled with the Spirit means that a person is under the influence of the Holy Spirit, so that his thoughts, words, and actions are controlled and ordered by God himself:

18. And be not drunk with wine, wherein is excess; but be filled with the Spirit;
19. Speaking to yourselves in psalms and hymns and spiritual songs, singing and making melody in your heart to the Lord;
20. Giving thanks always for all things unto God and the Father in the name of our Lord Jesus Christ;
21. Submitting yourselves one to another in the fear of God. (Eph. 5:18–21)

This was especially true of Micah: the Holy Spirit so filled him that he bubbled over with the word of God, which he could not but speak. A man thus filled with the Holy Spirit must speak the word that God has given him to speak. With that filling of the Spirit came power, judgment, and might (Mic. 3:8).

Power is the enabling strength of the Holy Spirit, who works in God's children holiness of life, soundness of mind, and in Micah the ability to exercise the office of prophet. The Holy Spirit does not give power to fall over, to knock others over, to laugh uncontrollably, or to behave like a fool.

Judgment was lacking in Judah, but Micah was filled with judgment, which means that he was filled with a zeal for right living according to God's law. Micah was faithful to God's word, which is the standard of righteousness, and he had a passion for justice. That is true of us too: we must be passionate about right and holy living, which is a sign that we are filled with the Holy Spirit.

Might is courage, a spiritual manliness that enabled Micah to swim against the tide of corruption, to go against the flow. He needed such courage because of his enemies and the enormously difficult task to preach the word to a people who hated it. Every Christian receives courage from the Spirit to live the Christian life.

Micah's ministry can be summed up with verse 8: "But truly I am full of power by the spirit of the LORD, and of judgment, and of might, to declare unto Jacob his transgression, and to Israel his sin." A Spirit-filled ministry is characterized by a bold, uncompromising declaration of truth. Micah's ministry was, especially at the beginning, largely negative, a task made doubly difficult by the false prophets who contradicted what he said. Micah was called to declare transgression and sin, a thankless but necessary task, to his own people, Jacob or Israel (Judah and Jerusalem).

That is, Micah's ministry was to preach against the sin of God's people. No wonder Micah needed to be filled with the Spirit, power, judgment, and might for that difficult task!

In his office of prophet, Micah is a type of Jesus Christ. All true prophets are types. When the people of Judah see and hear Micah, they must remember that the coming Messiah and Savior will also be a prophet (as well as the priest and the king). As the prophet of God, Jesus Christ was filled with the Holy Spirit: "For he whom God hath sent speaketh the words of God: for God giveth not the Spirit by measure unto him" (John 3:34). That means that God gave the Holy Spirit to Jesus Christ without limit, without measuring the Spirit out. This was possible because Jesus is the Son of God. We can only receive the Holy Spirit "by measure." Micah received the Holy Spirit "by measure." Jesus Christ received the Holy Spirit without measure.

Jesus, as the prophet of God, declared the word of God to Israel. Jesus indeed *is* the Word of God and has a perfect knowledge of God. Jesus dwells in the very bosom of God and therefore is perfectly equipped to make God known. Jesus never hesitated to declare to Israel her sins: Jesus is not a flattering, deceitful, venal prophet, but the true, faithful Word of God. Micah could say that he was filled with power, judgment, and might, but Jesus' power, judgment, and might brought him to this earth to suffer and die for sin.

Jesus might have used his power, judgment, and might to remain in heaven and destroy all mankind (including us) because of our sins. But that was not the will of our heavenly Father or the will of our Savior Jesus Christ.

Micah did not declare to Jacob and Israel her transgressions and sins merely so that she would feel bad about herself, or so that God might spoil the pleasure of sin in Judah and Jerusalem, but so that God's people among the Judeans and inhabitants of Jerusalem might be saved. There is no good news in a God of power, judgment, and might unless that power, judgment, and might are revealed in mercy, love, and grace. But mercy, love, and grace are never exercised at the expense of power, judgment, and might. That was the error of the venal prophets: Jehovah is only loving and merciful. Therefore, he will never punish Judah for sin. That was the false peace prophesied by the deceivers. The true message was Micah's: "Jehovah will show mercy only when his justice is truly satisfied. That will happen when the Messiah comes."

But to prepare you for the Messiah, you need to hear your sins. You need to understand your need. Otherwise you will never believe. Thus in power, judgment, and might Jesus died on the cross, bearing our sins, satisfying God's justice, and purchasing for us forgiveness. That is the message we need continually to hear. By God's grace a faithful pastor will preach it. Will you hear it?

FITTING JUDGMENT

Because the prophets had misused their office for financial gain, God will take his word from them. We must remember that in the Bible there are different kinds of false prophets. Four words in the text describe these false prophets: prophets, seers, and diviners, as well as priests.

There are the prophets described in Jeremiah 23:16–17:

16. Thus saith the Lord of hosts, Hearken not unto the words of the prophets that prophesy unto you: they make you vain: they speak a vision of their own heart, and not out of the mouth of the Lord.
17. They say still unto them that despise me, The Lord hath said, Ye shall have peace; and they say unto every one that walketh after the imagination of his own heart, No evil shall come upon you.

But there are also prophets who have a position among the people of God and who even have prophesied something true, although they themselves are false prophets (the classic examples are Balaam, Caiaphas, and Judas Iscariot). Some of these men may indeed have had a true vision of God in the past, and all of them had access to the scriptures. They had twisted God's word and used it for their own promotion. But most of them were simply liars who claimed to be prophets but were not.

God sends upon them a terrifying judgment, and that same judgment falls upon the people who reject the truth and willfully listen to the lie. It can be summed up in one word: darkness.

Darkness is the absence of, and the opposite of, light. Light is truth and salvation; darkness is ignorance, falsehood, and corruption. Micah 3:6 is filled with the judgment of darkness: "Night shall be unto you;" "It shall be dark unto you;" "The sun shall go down over the prophets, and the day shall be dark over them."

This means, concretely, that God will take away his word from the prophets and from those who listen to them. No matter what method they use (whether lawful or unlawful), God will not answer them: "Ye shall not have a vision...ye shall not divine" (v. 6); "There is no answer of God" (v. 7). Does God not do that in every age in the false church so that his word disappears and there is only darkness?

Take the Roman Catholic Church. There is a Bible in the Roman Catholic Church, but it is never read or preached except superficially, so that the people there are utterly ignorant of the truth. In addition, the doctrine preached in that false church is damnable heresy, not the truth of the gospel of Jesus Christ. Sadly, the evangelical churches are not far behind. When the word of God is replaced with entertainment, and when the people are not only ignorant, but happily ignorant, of truth, then you know that darkness has descended on the prophets:

11. Behold, the days come, saith the Lord God, that I will send a famine in the land, not a famine of bread, nor a thirst for water, but of hearing the words of the Lord:

12. And they shall wander from sea to sea, and from the north even to the east, they shall run to and fro to seek the word of the Lord, and shall not find it. (Amos 8:11–12)

10. And with all deceivableness of unrighteousness in them that perish; because they received not the love of the truth, that they might be saved.

11. And for this cause God shall send them strong delusion, that they should believe a lie:

12. That they all might be damned who believed not the truth, but had pleasure in unrighteousness. (2 Thess. 2:10–12)

The result of God's judgment upon the prophets will be shame; not shame that leads to sorrow over sin and repentance, but the shame of humiliation. When the Babylonians come, which the false prophets always denied, and the people come to the prophets, they will be ashamed. "What does God say about the Babylonians outside the gate?" the people will ask anxiously. The false prophets will be ashamed and will have nothing to say. This was not supposed to happen, according to their predictions. "Then shall the seers be ashamed, and the diviners confounded" (Mic. 3:7). Their optimistic, peaceful prophecies will be worthless in the day of God's judgment.

"They shall all cover their lips" (v. 7). That was a sign of leprosy and of mourning. The people will see how foolish they were to trust in the words of false prophets.

That will be the case for all false teachers in the church. The lies they promised never come, and neither they nor their followers will stand in the judgment. Only the gospel can prepare a man to face death with courage. A message of prosperity, easy believism, or moralistic pop-Christianity will fail on that day. What comfort can a false prophet offer a dying man?

We who know that Jesus is Lord, that Jesus is the savior from sin, even from our sins, will have light and joy on that day, because neither the Babylonian captivity nor death itself will separate us from the love of God. Do not be offended when the gospel exposes your sin, but instead repent of those sins and receive forgiveness in Jesus Christ.

Chapter 8

Zion's Kingdom Established in the Last Days

1. But in the last days it shall come to pass, that the mountain of the house of the Lord shall be established in the top of the mountains, and it shall be exalted above the hills; and people shall flow unto it.

2. And many nations shall come, and say, Come, and let us go up to the mountain of the Lord, and to the house of the God of Jacob; and he will teach us of his ways, and we will walk in his paths: for the law shall go forth of Zion, and the word of the Lord from Jerusalem.

3. And he shall judge among many people, and rebuke strong nations afar off; and they shall beat their swords into plowshares, and their spears into pruninghooks: nation shall not lift up a sword against nation, neither shall they learn war any more.

4. But they shall sit every man under his vine and under his fig tree; and none shall make them afraid: for the mouth of the Lord of hosts hath spoken it.

5. For all people will walk every one in the name of his god, and we will walk in the name of the Lord our God for ever and ever.

6. In that day, saith the Lord, will I assemble her that halteth, and I will gather her that is driven out, and her that I have afflicted;

7. And I will make her that halted a remnant, and her that was cast far off a strong nation: and the Lord shall reign over them in mount Zion from henceforth, even for ever.

8. And thou, O tower of the flock, the strong hold of the daughter of Zion, unto thee shall it come, even the first dominion; the kingdom shall come to the daughter of Jerusalem. (Micah 4:1–8)

In chapter 3:12, Micah prophesied the destruction of Jerusalem. That destruction would happen because of Judah's sins. Judah in Micah's day was apostate and had to be called to repentance. Judah's whole society was corrupt: there was no love for God or for the neighbor. As a result, Zion would be plowed as a field and reduced to rubble.

That judgment prophecy must have come as a terrible shock to the people, and it must have been awful for God's true children in the nation. If God destroyed Zion, what would become of God's promises in the covenant? If the temple was destroyed and the kings of David's line carried into captivity, how could the people worship God, and how could Christ come? It is to comfort God's people whom he has frightened that Micah preaches the message of chapters 4–5. Micah sees a day in the distant future when Zion will be restored. Isaiah had the same or a similar vision, which he recorded in Isaiah 2.

But notice that this vision is of the distant future. Not now, not even soon, declares Micah, Zion will like a phoenix rise from the ashes and rubble. This will happen in the last days. So Micah's prophecy is bittersweet: sweet because of what Micah promises, but bitter because Micah effectively says, "The salvation of

Jehovah will come to Zion, but you, the current generation, will not see it."

In fact, as we shall see, the future of Micah 4–5 is the New Testament age. *We* are living in the established kingdom of Zion. *We* are the many nations flowing into Zion. Christ is *our* king. Let us rejoice in Jehovah's salvation.

THE RESTORATION OF ZION

A restoration presupposes a fall from which to be restored. Micah 4:6 describes the fallen state of Zion, called the "daughter of Zion" or the "daughter of Jerusalem" in verse 8.

Zion has a threefold misery. First, she is called "her that halteth" (v. 6), that is, "she who walks with a limp." Second, she is called "her that was cast far off" (v. 7), that is, "she who was exiled or banished to a far country." Third, she is called "her that I have afflicted" (v. 6), that is, "she whom God has broken with calamitous judgments."

This misery has come upon the daughter of Zion as chastisement for Zion's sins. Micah prophesies here that this promise of hope, salvation, and restoration does not conflict with the previous prophecy of judgment.

Jerusalem will be chastised so severely that she will appear to be as a woman staggering with a limp, staggering through the rubble and weeping as she goes. Jerusalem will be sent far away into exile and broken, so that she is brought through the difficult way of chastisement to repentance. The majority of the nation will be destroyed so that the elect, chastened, and penitent remnant returns after the Babylonian captivity.

Zion's fall is described against the background of her former glory in verse 8. Zion or Jerusalem was (and will be again) the "tower of the flock" and "the strong hold of the daughter of Zion"

(v. 8). This curious expression refers to a lookout tower that a shepherd builds to watch over his sheep, which tower affords security and protection. In its heyday, Zion seemed to be invincible, for Jerusalem could not be conquered while God's blessing was upon it:

1. Great is the Lord, and greatly to be praised in the city of our God, in the mountain of his holiness.
2. Beautiful for situation, the joy of the whole earth, is mount Zion, on the sides of the north, the city of the great King.
3. God is known in her palaces for a refuge. (Ps. 48:1–3)

Nevertheless, once Jerusalem's people forsook Jehovah, they forfeited his blessing. This expression reminds God's people of how far they have fallen, but it also encourages them that they will rise again.

Zion's fall was slow but incremental. In the heyday of David and Solomon, Zion ruled over the whole nation and even subdued the surrounding nations. But Zion began to crumble with Solomon's idolatry and the defection of the ten tribes. The ten tribes apostatized and were destroyed, but the two tribes of Judah and Benjamin remained. They too over time fell from the faith. By the time Micah began his prophecy, Zion's days were numbered: she fell to Nebuchadnezzar and Babylon some one hundred and fifty years later.

Micah is not the only prophet to speak of the fall of Zion. Isaiah speaks of the stem of Jesse (Isa. 11:1), which means that David's kingdom is reduced to the stump of a tree, and Amos 9:11 speaks of David's fallen tabernacle.

To the limping, banished daughter of Zion broken by affliction, Jehovah promises a glorious restoration, a restoration more glorious than she had ever seen before. First, Micah 4:8 promises,

"Unto thee it shall come, even the first dominion." This means a reversal of the calamitous judgment endured by Zion in captivity. I will "assemble her that halteth...I will gather her that is driven out, and her that I have afflicted" (v. 6). "I will make her that halted a remnant, and her that was cast far off a strong nation" (v. 7). "The kingdom shall come to the daughter of Jerusalem" (v. 8).

Does, then, Micah promise here that Israel as a nation will be restored to her former glory so that the heyday of David and Solomon shall return? That is how many who read the prophets understand such promises. However, such a literalistic approach is fraught with difficulty and misses the point. After seventy years in Babylon, a limping, humbled remnant did return, and they did rebuild the temple, city, and walls, but that is only a very partial fulfillment of what Micah promises here.

If that was the fulfillment, it would be (quite frankly) disappointing. The temple was not as glorious as Solomon's temple, no Davidic king sat on David's earthly throne again, and Israel never enjoyed freedom and independence again. Therefore, some Christians believe that Micah's promise will be fulfilled later in a restored state of Israel, with a rebuilt temple in a literal earthly (millennial) kingdom.

But Micah is not promising a future millennial kingdom on earth. He is promising in the name of Jehovah the kingdom of Christ, and that is why we are interested in this prophecy. Without Christ this would have no significance for us, and a restored Israeli state with a rebuilt temple holds no charm for Christians who trust in the finished work of Christ and understand the New Testament as the fulfillment of the Old Testament.

When Micah promises that "the LORD shall reign over them in Mount Zion from henceforth, even for ever" (v. 7), he refers to the kingdom of Christ. Throughout the Old Testament a king is promised, who will come from the tribe of Judah, from the line of David, and he will rule forever. In these two chapters (Micah 4–5), the subject is especially the messianic kingdom of Jesus Christ in the New Testament age.

In Luke 1 the angel promises to Mary that her son will sit on the throne of David, which is where Jesus is now:

32. He shall be great, and shall be called the Son of the Highest: and the Lord God shall give unto him the throne of his father David:
33. And he shall reign over the house of Jacob for ever; and of his kingdom there shall be no end. (Luke 1:32–33)

30. Therefore being a prophet, and knowing that God had sworn with an oath to him, that of the fruit of his loins, according to the flesh, he would raise up Christ to sit on his throne;
31. He seeing this before spake of the resurrection of Christ, that his soul was not left in hell, neither his flesh did see corruption.
32. This Jesus hath God raised up, whereof we all are witnesses.
33. Therefore being by the right hand of God exalted, and having received of the Father the promise of the Holy Ghost, he hath shed forth this, which ye now see and hear. (Acts 2:30–33)

The kingdom of Christ as well as the throne of Christ is *heavenly*.

We need to bear something in mind. Micah was an Old Testament saint and prophet, and the only way in which he could explain the truth to his Old Testament audience was by means of the picture language of the Old Testament.

That is a key to understanding the prophets. They depicted

the truth using the brush strokes of an Old Testament artist, speaking of Zion, the temple, and other Old Testament realities in order to explain New Testament realities. But why did the prophets do this? Because the Old Testament saints could understand nothing else than this! If you try to teach a toddler with an encyclopedia, he will not understand. If a pastor tries to teach catechism to first graders, he must be careful to use pictorial language and not complicated theological concepts. Israel could never have understood, because they did not yet have the Holy Spirit, which meant that they were spiritually immature.

The Zion restored in Micah 4 is none other than the church of the New Testament. Study carefully the following passages:

13. And after they had held their peace, James answered, saying, Men and brethren, hearken unto me:
14. Simeon hath declared how God at the first did visit the Gentiles, to take out of them a people for his name.
15. And to this agree the words of the prophets; as it is written,
16. After this I will return, and will build again the tabernacle of David, which is fallen down; and I will build again the ruins thereof, and I will set it up:
17. That the residue of men might seek after the Lord, and all the Gentiles, upon whom my name is called, saith the Lord, who doeth all these things.
18. Known unto God are all his works from the beginning of the world.
19. Wherefore my sentence is, that we trouble not them, which from among the Gentiles are turned to God. (Acts 15:13–19)

But Jerusalem which is above is free, which is the mother of us all. (Gal. 4:26)

22. But ye are come unto mount Sion, and unto the city of the living God, the heavenly Jerusalem, and to an innumerable company of angels,

23. To the general assembly and church of the firstborn, which are written in heaven, and to God the Judge of all, and to the spirits of just men made perfect,

24. And to Jesus the mediator of the new covenant, and to the blood of sprinkling, that speaketh better things than that of Abel. (Heb. 12:22–24)

9. And there came unto me one of the seven angels which had the seven vials full of the seven last plagues, and talked with me, saying, Come hither, I will shew thee the bride, the Lamb's wife.

10. And he carried me away in the spirit to a great and high mountain, and shewed me that great city, the holy Jerusalem, descending out of heaven from God. (Rev. 21:9–10)

In other words, Micah prophesies of the New Testament kingdom of Jesus Christ under the typology of Old Testament Zion.

THE EXALTATION OF ZION

God is not satisfied with a mere restoration of Zion, for he will exalt her so that she becomes higher than every other mountain (Mic. 4:1). Micah describes this in terms of a geological miracle, an upheaval of the mountain itself so that it is physically higher than every other mountain. At the top of that mountain the temple of God will be exalted, and all nations shall flow to that mountain to seek Jehovah.

If we take this literally, Zion and Jerusalem would have to be lifted up to a greater elevation than Mount Everest in the Hima-layas. We know that this has never happened. It did not happen in the Old Testament when the people returned from Babylon, and Zion is still at the same elevation today. Therefore, we ask, will this happen literally in the future? Some say it will take place during the millennium, but we reject that view as foolishness.

There are other "mountain prophecies" that none expect to happen literally. In Isaiah 40:4 the prophet declares, "Every valley shall be exalted, and every mountain and hill shall be made low." That prophecy was fulfilled in the days of John the Baptist. Nobody expected that to happen literally, and it never did. Speaking of the days of Zerubbabel, the prophet Zechariah announces, "Who art thou, O great mountain? before Zerubbabel thou shalt become a plain" (Zech. 4:7). In that day, no mountain was literally flattened. Even so there will be no future literal fulfillment of Micah 4:1.

In fact, the exaltation promised in Micah 4 is a *spiritual* exaltation. Zion will become spiritually prominent, not geo-graphically, geologically, or politically prominent. A literal fulfillment would require the building of a new temple (the last one was destroyed in AD 70), but the New Testament rules out a future temple. It does that by teaching us that there is no more offering for sin because of the perfect atonement of Jesus Christ. A future temple would mean reinstituted sacrifices of which the New Testament knows nothing. Instead, the New Testament teaches us that God is building a temple in the New Testament age, the church made up of Jews and Gentiles who believe in Jesus Christ:

> Know ye not that ye are the temple of God, and that the Spirit of God dwelleth in you? (1 Cor. 3:16)

> And what agreement hath the temple of God with idols? for ye are the temple of the living God; as God hath said,

I will dwell in them, and walk in them; and I will be their God, and they shall be my people. (2 Cor. 6:16)

19. Now therefore ye are no more strangers and foreign-ers, but fellow-citizens with the saints, and of the household of God;
20. And are built upon the foundation of the apostles and prophets, Jesus Christ himself being the chief corner stone;
21. In whom all the building fitly framed together groweth unto an holy temple in the Lord:
22. In whom ye also are builded together for an habitation of God through the Spirit. (Eph. 2:19–22)

Therefore, we do not look for a future elevation of the geo-logical structure known as Mount Zion, but we understand that Zion is exalted to heaven itself. In the New Testament age, Zion or the church attracts through her preaching of the gospel peo-ple from every nation in which God effectually calls sinners unto himself.

That is how Micah describes it. Chapter 4:1 says that "peo-ple[s] shall flow unto it," and verse 2 declares that "many nations shall come." Verse 2 adds, "For the law shall go forth of Zion." The exaltation of Zion, therefore, consists in her becoming the center of worship for God's people so that one church is ruled by Christ by his word and Holy Spirit.

We notice yet again that all this is described using the lan-guage of Old Testament typology. If you wanted to describe the catholic church of Jews and Gentiles to an Old Testament Jew, what language would you use? You would employ the language Micah uses here! For the Old Testament Jew, the worship of God was unthinkable without Jerusalem and the temple. If you had said to one of Micah's believing contemporaries, "In the future

God will gather believers from all the nations of the Gentiles," that would have confused and even disturbed him. If you had added, "The Gentiles will worship in their own nations, and the Holy Spirit will dwell in each local assembly and in the hearts of the people, and there will be no temple or Israel as we see today," they would have looked at you with astonishment.

"But what about Zion? What about the temple? What about the sacrifices, priests, and incense?" Before Christ's coming it never would have made any sense. Indeed, the early church had difficulty understanding it. Therefore, Micah accommodates to the people's understanding.

Perhaps we can illustrate it with an example of our time. If, hypothetically, you could travel back in time to the days of Augustine, how would you explain a modern Reformed worship service to one of the church members of that day? "I am from the Protestant Reformed Churches." "I am from the Covenant Protestant Reformed Church." "I am from the Limerick Reformed Fellowship." How would a man from Augustine's day understand that? He would have no concept of "Protestant" (there were no Protestants in Augustine's day). He would have no concept of "Reformed" (the Reformation would not take place for over a millennium). Imagine, in addition, that you tried to explain to such a fourth- or fifth-century saint that your worship service will be "live streamed," or that you offered him a CD of last week's sermon. He would have looked at you in utter astonishment! He would not have the concepts to understand what you meant. How much more is this not the case with respect to explaining New Testament messianic salvation to the Old Testament saints!

How, then, do you explain the fullness of New Testament messianic salvation using Old Testament picture language? First, the peoples of the earth will flow to Jerusalem and will become believers in Jehovah when Zion becomes the center of the earth.

Second, the law will go forth out of Zion and the word of God from Jerusalem. Third, the Gentiles will be taught the ways of Jehovah because from the heart this is what they will desire. That is an amazing prophecy! God will save the Gentiles, and he will give them new hearts by which they love and seek him!

Christ is the king promised in this chapter. He is sharply contrasted with the leaders of Judah in Micah's day. Christ shall teach the Gentiles Jehovah's ways. The false prophets and priests of Micah's day had ceased to teach truth. They will be swept away in judgment, and Jesus himself shall teach. He will do this by the preaching of the gospel in the New Testament age.

Christ shall judge among many people and rebuke strong nations (v. 3). Judgment and rebuke here have the meaning of settling disputes and giving justice. Judgment and justice, as we saw in chapters 2–3, were absent in Jerusalem. The result of Jesus' judgment will be to subdue rebels to himself so that they willingly and gladly serve him from the heart. That is happening in the church.

On the basis of the righteousness of Zion's king, we (both Jews and Gentiles) flow into the kingdom of God. No sinner can enter into the kingdom of God without the forgiveness of sins. What good is it to learn the law of God if the law simply teaches us what God demands but does not give strength to obey? What good is it to see in the law my own condemnation? All the law can teach us is that God is holy, that we are sinful, and that we must be punished. Therefore, we must remember that Zion's king fulfilled righteousness for us.

On the cross the perfect demands of Jehovah were met. There Christ offered a perfect sacrifice by offering himself. Christ alone was qualified to offer such a sacrifice because he is a real, sinless man and because he is God. In love he took our guilt and shame. Thus God's wrath is satisfied: there is a righteous basis for our being citizens.

THE BLESSEDNESS OF ZION

Zion's blessedness can be summed up in one word: peace. We notice that this peace is described in terms of Old Testament typology.

There will be reconciliation between nations. In the Old Testament, Israel was always at war with other nations who threatened her, and other nations were at war with Israel. That will cease. Warfare in the Old Testament was fought with swords, but "nation shall not lift up sword against nation" (Mic. 4:3). So distant will war be from the nations in the messianic age that they will not learn it, and their weapons will become agricultural implements: "They shall beat their swords into plowshares, and their spears into pruninghooks" (v. 3).

A literal fulfillment of this prophecy has never occurred in the past, and we should not expect it in the future either. In fact, the New Testament makes clear that warfare among the ungodly nations of the world will be normal and even increase throughout the entire New Testament age:

6. And ye shall hear of wars and rumours of wars: see that ye be not troubled: for all these things must come to pass, but the end is not yet.

7. For nation shall rise against nation, and kingdom against kingdom: and there shall be famines, and pestilences, and earthquakes, in divers places. (Matt. 24:6–7)

And there went out another horse that was red: and power was given to him that sat thereon to take peace from the earth, and that they should kill one another: and there was given unto him a great sword. (Rev. 6:4)

Peace will not be achieved as a result of international peace treaties. There is no peace for the wicked. Therefore, the world's dreams of peace without righteousness will never be realized.

If this prophecy happened literally, we would be back in the preindustrial age. Modern nations arm their military with much more sophisticated weapons than "swords." No radical literalist really teaches that in the future the world's military powers will employ swords, which they will then beat into plowshares. Modern agriculture does not use plowshares. Swords and plowshares (as opposed to armored tanks, ballistic missiles, tractors, combine harvesters, and the like) belong in the preindustrial age.

The peace promised here is better and more fundamental than earthly peace: it is the peace created and preserved by Christ in his church.

The other blessing is related to the peace: it is security and freedom from fear. What in the Old Testament is the most idyllic picture of such peace and security? Verse 4 provides the answer, for each man will "sit under his vine and fig tree." Does this mean that in the future everyone will literally have a vine and fig tree of his own to sit under? No; this is Old Testament picture language again.

An Old Testament saint would immediately think of Solomon's reign: "And Judah and Israel dwelt safely, every man under his vine and under his fig tree, from Dan even to Beersheba, all the days of Solomon" (1 Kings 4:25). The kingdom of the Messiah will be like the reign of a restored and exalted Solomon. Peace will be enjoyed, a peace so secure that a man will be able to sit under his own fig tree and vine without fear. This will be the fruit of the coming of Jesus the Messiah. The peace between the nations will occur when men, women, and children from every nation are reconciled to God by the blood of Christ.

The reason for a lack of peace is sin: hostility of man for God and his neighbor. So long as sin remains, there is no peace. Even if man achieves a ceasefire for a while, sin (greed, selfishness, envy, and so on) will cause war to start again (James 4:1–2).

Moreover, the war in the Old Testament was between Israel and the Gentiles. Micah prophesies of a time when the Gentiles will lay down their weapons and be reconciled to the Jews and worship Zion's God. That happened, Ephesians 2:14 tells us, in the cross of Christ. In him, Jews and Gentiles together are reconciled to God in one church.

There is only one question left for us to answer: when shall this be? Micah sees this in his future from the vantage point of an Old Testament prophet. The answer is "in the last days" (Mic. 4:1) and "in that day" (vv. 6–7). The New Testament teaches us that the last days began with the coming of Christ and that they shall end with the second coming:

16. But this is that which was spoken by the prophet Joel;

17. And it shall come to pass in the last days, saith God, I will pour out of my Spirit upon all flesh: and your sons and your daughters shall prophesy, and your young men shall see visions, and your old men shall dream dreams:

18. And on my servants and on my handmaidens I will pour out in those days of my Spirit; and they shall prophesy. (Acts 2:16–18)

Now all these things happened unto them for ensamples: and they are written for our admonition, upon whom the ends of the world are come. (1 Cor. 10:11)

1. God, who at sundry times and in divers manners spake in time past unto the fathers by the prophets,

2. Hath in these last days spoken unto us by his Son, whom he hath appointed heir of all things, by whom also he made the worlds. (Heb. 1:1–2)

The kingdom promised in Micah 4, therefore, has come. It was inaugurated in the incarnation, death, resurrection, and ascension of Jesus Christ. Throughout the New Testament age, God's elect, from both Jews and Gentiles, are gathered into it. It comes not by political power but as the gospel is preached: "The law shall go forth of Zion, and the word of the LORD from Jerusalem" (Mic. 4:2). It manifests itself in faithful, Christian churches of which we with our children are called to be lively members. And the consummation and perfection of the kingdom will take place when Jesus Christ returns.

Chapter 9

Zion's Messianic Birth Pangs

9. Now why dost thou cry out aloud? is there no king in thee? is thy counsellor perished? for pangs have taken thee as a woman in travail.

10. Be in pain, and labour to bring forth, O daughter of Zion, like a woman in travail: for now shalt thou go forth out of the city, and thou shalt dwell in the field, and thou shalt go even to Babylon; there shalt thou be delivered; there the Lord shall redeem thee from the hand of thine enemies.

11. Now also many nations are gathered against thee, that say, Let her be defiled, and let our eye look upon Zion.

12. But they know not the thoughts of the Lord, neither understand they his counsel: for he shall gather them as the sheaves into the floor.

13. Arise and thresh, O daughter of Zion: for I will make thine horn iron, and I will make thy hoofs brass: and thou shalt beat in pieces many people: and I will consecrate their gain unto the Lord, and their substance unto the Lord of the whole earth.

1. Now gather thyself in troops, O daughter of troops: he hath laid siege against us: they shall smite the judge of Israel with a rod upon the cheek.
2. But thou, Bethlehem Ephratah, though thou be little among the thousands of Judah, yet out of thee shall he come forth unto me that is to be ruler in Israel; whose goings forth have been from of old, from everlasting.
3. Therefore will he give them up, until the time that she which travaileth hath brought forth: then the remnant of his brethren shall return unto the children of Israel. (Micah 4:9–5:3)

Micah is a prophet of abrupt contrasts: he moves rapidly between judgment and mercy. He did that in chapter 2, in which he warned the people that Jehovah would dispossess them, whereupon almost without any transition he prophesies of the breaker, Jesus Christ. He does that again in chapters 4–5. At the end of chapter 3, he prophesies the utter ruin of Jerusalem, whereupon, again immediately afterward, he completely reverses Jerusalem's ruin with a prophecy of Zion's future last-days exaltation. We saw in the previous chapter that Zion's exaltation and peace are an Old Testament typical description of the New Testament age of Christ when Jews and Gentiles will be gathered into one church.

Having dazzled the people with the glory of Zion's restored and exalted kingdom, Micah drags us abruptly back to the "now" of the more immediate future. Zion's children are encouraged, but they must wait before the kingdom comes. In fact, Zion did not know this, but she would have to wait for another seven hundred years.

The coming of Christ promised in Micah's prophecy would be preceded by many afflictions. Zion's children needed to be prepared for that. With God—as then, so now—there are no shortcuts.

One figure dominates our text, and that figure really explains Old Testament history. The figure is of a pregnant woman in labor, a woman in travail. Zion is that pregnant woman, and her labor pains are her desperate attempt to bring forth the Christ, the Messiah. Thus we can understand them as messianic birth pangs.

THE IDEA

In the latter half of chapter 4, Micah prophesies affliction for Zion, but a particular kind of affliction: birth pangs.

> 9. Now why dost thou cry out aloud? is there no king in thee? is thy counsellor perished? for pangs have taken thee as a woman in travail.
> 10. Be in pain, and labour to bring forth, O daughter of Zion, like a woman in travail: for now shalt thou go forth out of the city, and thou shalt dwell in the field, and thou shalt go even to Babylon; there shalt thou be delivered; there the Lord shall redeem thee from the hand of thine enemies. (4:9–10)

> Therefore will he give them up, until the time that she which travaileth hath brought forth: then the remnant of his brethren shall return unto the children of Israel. (5:3)

Birth pangs are unique among pains. Birth pangs are sharp and sudden.

First, they are sharp. Birth pangs are powerful contractions of the muscles of the womb to bring about the birth of the baby. Micah warns Zion that sharp, painful contractions will come upon her: "Pangs have taken thee...Be in pain, and labour to bring forth" (4:9–10).

Second, they are sudden. Although a pregnant woman has a reasonable idea about her due date, the pangs themselves come upon her suddenly and without warning. She may have anticipated them, but she is never really ready for them. The terrible afflictions that Zion will experience will be unexpected. Many (most) in Zion will be thoroughly unprepared for them despite the warnings of the prophets.

Birth pangs are also debilitating or incapacitating. So sharp are birth pangs that they make a woman double over in pain. Micah declares, "Be in pain" (v. 10), and "Pangs have taken thee as a woman in travail" (v. 9). The Bible often describes the paralyzing fear of the wicked as birth pangs: "Ask ye now, and see whether a man doth travail with child? wherefore do I see every man with his hands on his loins, as a woman in travail, and all faces are turned into paleness?" (Jer. 30:6).

In addition, birth pangs are intensifying, that is, they increase in severity as the birth approaches. When a woman goes into labor, she measures the intervals between contractions. When the contractions are frequent enough, she usually gets ready to go to the hospital. The closer the birth, the closer together are the pangs, and the more powerful the contractions. Micah prophesies a history of affliction for Judah increasing in severity as the day approaches.

Most importantly, birth pangs are harbingers of hope and salvation. Birth pangs signal the coming of a child into the world. Birth pangs are not pointless, fruitless, purposeless tortures, but they issue in a happy ending. That is why the mother is able to endure them: with each contraction and with each push, she says, "The baby is coming. I am almost there. Soon I will be holding my baby." Jesus said, "A woman when she is in travail hath sorrow, because her hour is come: but as soon as she is delivered of the child, she remembereth no more the anguish, for joy that a man is born into the world" (John 16:21).

Thus Micah's prophecy is a prophecy of hope for Zion, who will have a long history of sharp, sudden, incapacitating, intensifying afflictions. But through them all she will be preserved, and the outcome of these birth pangs will be the birth of the Messiah and of the messianic age as described in chapters 4–5. This must have comforted the elect remnant, the true Israel within the nation, and this must comfort us, who are the children of Abraham through faith in Jesus Christ.

What does that motif of birth pangs in scripture mean? First, birth pangs represent the horror that grips the wicked when sudden destruction comes upon them:

> They shall be afraid: pangs and sorrows shall take hold of them; they shall be in pain as a woman that travaileth: they shall be amazed one at another; their faces shall be as flames. (Isa. 13:8)

> For when they shall say, Peace and safety; then sudden destruction cometh upon them, as travail upon a woman with child; and they shall not escape. (1 Thess. 5:3)

Second, birth pangs represent the convulsions of the creation as it labors to bring forth the day of the Lord:

> 6. And ye shall hear of wars and rumours of wars: see that ye be not troubled: for all these things must come to pass, but the end is not yet.
> 7. For nation shall rise against nation, and kingdom against kingdom: and there shall be famines, and pestilences, and earthquakes, in divers places.
> 8. All these are the beginning of sorrows. (Matt. 24:6–8)

> 20. For the creature was made subject to vanity, not willingly, but by reason of him who hath subjected the same in hope,

21. Because the creature itself also shall be delivered from the bondage of corruption into the glorious liberty of the children of God.
22. For we know that the whole creation groaneth and travaileth in pain together until now.
23. And not only they, but ourselves also, which have the firstfruits of the Spirit, even we ourselves groan within ourselves, waiting for the adoption, to wit, the redemption of our body. (Rom. 8:20–23)

Third, birth pangs represent the effort with which pastors agonize over the souls of people, especially over those who are going astray doctrinally or in their walk. "My little children, of whom I travail in birth again until Christ be formed in you, I desire to be present with you now, and to change my voice; for I stand in doubt of you" (Gal. 4:19–20). Micah, no doubt, agonized over the souls of Zion in this way (Mic. 1:8–9).

Fourth, the coming forth of Christ from the grave is described as birth pangs: "Whom God hath raised up, having loosed the pains of death: because it was not possible that he should be holden of it" (Acts 2:24).

While all these points are true and valid, the idea in Micah 4–5 is very specific: the birth pangs of Zion are her pains to bring forth the promised Messiah, Jesus Christ. In a certain sense, Zion, as a pregnant mother, was in labor to bring forth Christ throughout the Old Testament, which history is the account of some four thousand years of painful labor. This is the teaching of Revelation 12:2, where God's Old Testament people are depicted as a woman "travailing in birth, and pained to be delivered."

This was the longest gestation period in history. The pregnancy really began in the garden of Eden, where God said, "I will put enmity between thee and the woman, and between thy seed and her seed; it shall bruise thy head, and thou shalt bruise his heel" (Gen. 3:15). All of the afflictions of the Old Testament people of God were birth pangs: the murder of Abel, the flood, the four hundred years of bondage in Egypt, the wilderness wanderings, the trials under the judges, and the division of the kingdom were all birth pangs. Although Micah gives Zion a glimpse of the messianic age after she will have given birth to the Messiah, Micah warns Zion that there are more birth pangs to come.

These afflictions are necessary to humble Zion, to chastise her, to purify her, and to prepare her for the coming of Christ. The hard labor and the incapacitating birth pangs will be worth it, but at the end it must be clear that Zion could never have brought forth Christ except by the grace of God. Zion must not be able to boast that she brought forth her own salvation. God will not allow that. That is why he will make the birth pangs of Zion so severe that her salvation will again and again seem to be entirely impossible. Time and time again the church will be in danger of miscarrying:

> 17. Like as a woman with child, that draweth near the time of her delivery, is in pain, and crieth out in her pangs; so have we been in thy sight, O Lord.
> 18. We have been with child, we have been in pain, we have as it were brought forth wind; we have not wrought any deliverance in the earth; neither have the inhabitants of the world fallen. (Isa. 26:17–18)

And they said unto him, Thus saith Hezekiah, This day is a day of trouble, and of rebuke, and of blasphemy: for the children are come to the birth, and there is not strength to bring forth. (37:3)

In fact, by the time the church actually brings forth Christ, the line of David will be reduced to a virgin and the Christ will have to come by a miracle.

THE EXAMPLES

We have seen generally the meaning of the passage and the main idea behind the prophecy. Now we are ready to look at the details. Micah in chapter 4:1–8 has spoken about "the last days" (v. 1) and "that day" (v. 6). The last days are the days of the New Testament messianic age, the days in which we live.

From the future glories of the messianic kingdom, Micah brings Zion back to earth with a thud. He does so with that word *now*. "Now" does not mean right now but refers to the nearer future. It does not refer to the "last days" or to "that day" (the prophets' way of designating the New Testament age), but to a time coming soon. Four times Micah uses the word *now* in the passage before us: "Now why dost thou cry out aloud?" (v. 9); "Now shalt thou go forth out of the city" (v. 10); "Now also many nations are gathered against thee" (v. 11); and "Now gather thyself in troops, O daughter of troops" (5:1).

Effectively, Micah is warning Judah, "Do not get carried away by my latter-days prophecy, because that future glory does not mean that life will be easy from this point. There are many afflictions ahead, and you must be prepared for them."

Micah then describes three future events, three painful birth pangs in Zion's immediate or near future.

The first is the Babylonian captivity, which happened about one hundred and fifty years after Micah. Micah sees a day in the future when Zion will have no king to protect her, or at least no king strong enough to protect her from her enemies: "Now why dost thou cry out aloud? is there no king in thee? is thy counsellor perished?" (4:9). This is a sharp and sudden contrast from verse 8, where "the first dominion" and "the kingdom" are promised to Zion.

Before God's promise can be fulfilled in Jesus Christ, the Davidic kingdom as Micah's contemporaries knew it must fall. That is a terrible blow because the Davidic kingdom is necessary for the coming of Christ. Because of the loss of Zion's king, she will suffer indignity and misery in Babylon. She will go forth out of the city, which is a sharp birth pang, for how shall she survive if she is not in the promised land where God dwells? She will dwell in the field: without shelter or protection, forsaken, and forlorn. And she will go to Babylon: this will be a terrible contraction, which will shake Zion to her core. Babylon, the wicked, idolatrous, pagan nation, will capture Zion, God's people, God's bride! This is also remarkable because when Micah prophesied Babylon was not yet a world power. Assyria was the dominant world power of that day.

The second affliction is to be surrounded by her enemies. This time Micah does not specify who the enemies are or when this shall take place. Such a situation has occurred repeatedly in Zion's history and, warns Micah, will happen again.

The imagery is very graphic: a helpless woman surrounded by a crowd of cruel men, whose intention is to defile her. They gloat upon her as they see her helplessness: "Let her be defiled... let our eye look upon Zion" (v. 11). That is the desire of the wicked: they hate her because she is holy, and so they desire to defile her. This vision is representative of the many times when the wicked nations have surrounded God's people and all hope appeared to be lost. As Zion looks about her, she is overcome with another debilitating, incapacitating birth pang. The prophets frequently speak of this:

1. For, behold, in those days, and in that time, when I shall bring again the captivity of Judah and Jerusalem,

2. I will also gather all nations, and will bring them down into the valley of Jehoshaphat, and will plead with them there for my people and for my heritage Israel, whom they have scattered among the nations, and parted my land…

11. Assemble yourselves, and come, all ye heathen, and gather yourselves together round about: thither cause thy mighty ones to come down, O Lord.

12. Let the heathen be wakened, and come up to the valley of Jehoshaphat: for there will I sit to judge all the heathen round about.

13. Put ye in the sickle, for the harvest is ripe: come, get you down; for the press is full, the vats overflow; for their wickedness is great.

14. Multitudes, multitudes in the valley of decision: for the day of the Lord is near in the valley of decision. (Joel 3:1–2, 11–14)

2. Behold, I will make Jerusalem a cup of trembling unto all the people round about, when they shall be in the siege both against Judah and against Jerusalem.

3. And in that day will I make Jerusalem a burdensome stone for all people: all that burden themselves with it shall be cut in pieces, though all the people of the earth be gathered together against it. (Zech. 12:2–3)

1. Behold, the day of the Lord cometh, and thy spoil shall be divided in the midst of thee.

2. For I will gather all nations against Jerusalem to battle; and the city shall be taken, and the houses rifled, and

the women ravished; and half of the city shall go forth into captivity, and the residue of the people shall not be cut off from the city.

3. Then shall the Lord go forth, and fight against those nations, as when he fought in the day of battle.

4. And his feet shall stand in that day upon the mount of Olives, which is before Jerusalem on the east, and the mount of Olives shall cleave in the midst thereof toward the east and toward the west, and there shall be a very great valley; and half of the mountain shall remove toward the north, and half of it toward the south.

5. And ye shall flee to the valley of the mountains; for the valley of the mountains shall reach unto Azal: yea, ye shall flee, like as ye fled from before the earthquake in the days of Uzziah king of Judah: and the Lord my God shall come, and all the saints with thee. (14:1–5)

Other examples include the book of Esther (when Haman masterminded a plot to exterminate the Jews) and the history of the intertestamental period (during which history the Syrians, the Greeks, and the Romans all surrounded Zion at one time or another to destroy her).

Indeed, the same motif is found in the book of Revelation to describe Satan's last onslaught against the church:

And he gathered them together into a place called in the Hebrew tongue Armageddon. (Rev. 16:16)

7. And when the thousand years are expired, Satan shall be loosed out of his prison,

8. And shall go out to deceive the nations which are in the four quarters of the earth, Gog and Magog, to

gather them together to battle: the number of whom is as the sand of the sea.

9. And they went up on the breadth of the earth, and compassed the camp of the saints about, and the beloved city: and fire came down from God out of heaven, and devoured them. (20:7–9)

The third affliction is a siege: "He hath laid siege against us" (Mic. 5:1). This is similar to the affliction mentioned earlier, and again Micah does not specify which siege is meant; Zion would be besieged multiple times. Zion is commanded to gather herself together to defend herself: "Now gather thyself in troops, O daughter of troops" (v. 1). The idea is that Zion has only a few soldiers, for a troop is a small raiding band, not a strong army. Defending herself in such a case is vanity. In fact, the result of the siege is utter humiliation for Zion's king: "They shall smite the judge of Israel with a rod upon the cheek" (v. 1). Another king will have Zion's king in his power and will be able to slap him on the face.

This history of affliction will continue until the coming of the Messiah. Perhaps Micah is describing most directly the siege of Jerusalem by Sennacherib in the days of Hezekiah, or he is describing the last king of Judah, Zedekiah (2 Kings 25:4–7). Those sieges are significant, but they do not exhaust this prophecy. God will give Zion up to many such afflictions and chastisements. Then when she who travails has brought forth, the church shall be gathered: "The remnant of his brethren shall return unto the children of Israel" (Mic. 5:3).

THE OUTCOME

Micah 4–5 contains some remarkable prophecies of salvation. First, from Babylon Jehovah promises deliverance and redemption. Notice how the prophet stresses the word "there" in 4:10:

"*there* shalt thou be delivered...*there* the LORD shall redeem thee" (emphasis added). Deliverance and redemption will happen in Babylon itself, the place you would least expect Jehovah to save his people. The deliverance of verse 10 will be like the deliverance of Exodus 3:8: "And I am come down to deliver them out of the hand of the Egyptians, and to bring them up out of that land unto a good land and a large, unto a land flowing with milk and honey."

Redemption is an important word in the concept of salvation. To redeem, Jehovah enters into a relationship with the people he redeems. The right to redeem was, under the law, only possible to a near kinsman, which truth is beautifully illustrated in the story of Ruth. In order to redeem us, Jehovah became one of us, a man, and as a man Jehovah pays a price for our redemption, which is his own life:

14. Forasmuch then as the children are partakers of flesh and blood, he also himself likewise took part of the same; that through death he might destroy him that had the power of death, that is, the devil;
15. And deliver them who through fear of death were all their lifetime subject to bondage.
16. For verily he took not on him the nature of angels; but he took on him the seed of Abraham.
17. Wherefore in all things it behoved him to be made like unto his brethren, that he might be a merciful and faithful high priest in things pertaining to God, to make reconciliation for the sins of the people. (Heb. 2:14–17)

Second, Jehovah will turn the tables on the enemies who surround Zion. They imagine that they have come together to destroy Zion, but they do not know that Jehovah himself has gathered them for a very different purpose: their destruction. Jehovah has a plan for his enemies, the enemies of his people. He has thoughts, but they are not thoughts of peace, prosperity, and salvation. The wicked, fools that they are, do not perceive Jehovah's plans.

Micah graphically describes the outcome both for the wicked and for Zion. All the antagonists are gathered on Jehovah's threshing floor, where the wheat was beaten to separate the grain from the chaff. Animals were used to tread out the wheat. Here the animal is Zion, for she is like an ox or an heifer, and God gives her power to crush her enemies: "I will make thine horn iron, and I will make thy hoofs brass: and thou shalt beat in pieces many people" (Mic. 4:13).

This will be done to the glory of God: the spoil of the enemies will be utterly destroyed in dedication to Jehovah.

14. Fear not, thou worm Jacob, and ye men of Israel; I will help thee, saith the Lord, and thy redeemer, the Holy One of Israel.
15. Behold, I will make thee a new sharp threshing instrument having teeth: thou shalt thresh the mountains, and beat them small, and shalt make the hills as chaff.
16. Thou shalt fan them, and the wind shall carry them away, and the whirlwind shall scatter them: and thou shalt rejoice in the Lord, and shalt glory in the Holy One of Israel. (Isa. 41:14–16)

For thus saith the LORD of hosts, the God of Israel; The daughter of Babylon is like a threshingfloor, it is time to thresh her: yet a little while, and the time of her harvest shall come. (Jer. 51:33)

Whose fan is in his hand, and he will throughly purge his floor, and gather his wheat into the garner; but he will burn up the chaff with unquenchable fire. (Matt. 3:12)

18. And another angel came out from the altar, which had power over fire; and cried with a loud cry to him that had the sharp sickle, saying, Thrust in thy sharp sickle, and gather the clusters of the vine of the earth; for her grapes are fully ripe.
19. And the angel thrust in his sickle into the earth, and gathered the vine of the earth, and cast it into the great winepress of the wrath of God.
20. And the winepress was trodden without the city, and blood came out of the winepress, even unto the horse bridles, by the space of a thousand and six hundred furlongs. (Rev.14:18–20)

The third deliverance (from the siege in Micah 5:1) is the birth of the Messiah in verse 2, which is the subject of the next chapter.

Zion's triumph, described here under certain graphic pictures, happens at the cross. All Zion's birth pangs are leading to the cross, where Christ will die for our sins. Zion will not miscarry, for Jehovah will miraculously bring forth the promised Messiah. He even promises the birthplace in verse 2. The Christ who was promised will come, and he will come for one purpose: to suffer and die for his people so that they can inherit the promised kingdom.

At the cross the enemy (Satan and his seed) is decisively crushed and destroyed. Neither the Old Testament Zion nor the New Testament church destroys her enemies by brute force. Revelation 12 tells us, "They overcame him by the blood of the lamb" (v. 11). By the blood of the Lamb, Satan and all the wicked are defeated. Zion is delivered and redeemed at the cross. The price to set us free from our sins was paid there, for the Son of God became man, assumed our nature and our guilt, and took our punishment. There the judge of Israel was smitten with a rod

upon his cheek. He was publicly and shamefully brought to condemnation and death. Although he was innocent, he underwent
shame and suffering for us:

63. And the men that held Jesus mocked him, and smote
    him.
64. And when they had blindfolded him, they struck him
    on the face, and asked him, saying, Prophesy, who is it
    that smote thee?
65. And many other things blasphemously spake they
    against him. (Luke 22:63–65)

The fruit of Christ's death is that the church of both the Old
Testament and the New Testament is saved: "The remnant of
his brethren shall return unto the children of Israel" (Mic. 5:3).
We are Christ's brethren. In the Old Testament, the majority of
Christ's brethren were found among the Jews, but that changed
dramatically in the New Testament. Ethnicity and bloodlines
do not determine kinship with Christ. Election determines
who Christ's brethren are, and faith, worked into Christ's brethren by the operation of the Holy Spirit, unites the elect to him.
Therefore, it does not matter if you are of the tribe of Benjamin
or Judah, or if you are a Gentile. What matters is faith in Christ,
for if you believe in him you can know and must know that you
belong to Christ's brethren.

We are gathered unto Christ; we are engrafted into the one
olive tree; we are made branches in the true vine; and we are
incorporated into the spiritual temple of God. We are the children of Israel according to God's promise. Listen to the beautiful
words of Hebrews 2:11–13:

11. For both he that sanctifieth and they who are sancti-
    fied are all of one: for which cause he is not ashamed
    to call them brethren,

12. Saying, I will declare thy name unto my brethren, in the midst of the church will I sing praise unto thee.
13. And again, I will put my trust in him. And again, Behold I and the children which God hath given me.

Therefore, Micah's message is for us, just as it was for Judah. The life of the believer is long and hard, and every affliction is like a birth pang promising the birth of a better age. But take heart; the pangs, although sharp now, are worth it. Christ is coming, and when he comes we will be able to confess that all the trials we experienced were necessary to prepare us for that day. "For I reckon that the sufferings of this present time are not worthy to be compared with the glory which shall be revealed in us" (Rom. 8:18).

Chapter 10

Jehovah's Ruler from Bethlehem-Judah

But thou, Bethlehem Ephratah, though thou be little among the thousands of Judah, yet out of thee shall he come forth unto me that is to be ruler in Israel; whose goings forth have been from of old, from everlasting. (Micah 5:2)

In the previous chapter, we saw that Micah prophesied of Israel's future in terms of birth pangs. We saw that the goal of Zion's pregnancy, labor, and birth pangs was the birth of Christ. Micah employs rich imagery to prepare Zion for difficult years of affliction. But Jehovah would redeem Zion from Babylon (4:10), from all the enemy nations (4:12–13), from a siege (5:1–3), and ultimately from her sins. The result would be the coming of the Messiah and the gathering of God's people, who, as we have seen, include elect Jews and Gentiles.

In the midst of that prophecy (4:9–5:3) Micah prophesies specifically about the Messiah's birth. Micah 5:2 is unique in Old Testament prophecy because it specifies the birthplace of the Messiah. To us, the prophecy of Bethlehem is warm, comforting, and familiar, but to Micah's contemporaries it was a surprise.

That the Messiah will be born in Bethlehem is very significant. It means that he will not be born in the palace in Jerusalem, and it spells disaster for the Davidic dynasty of Judah. This prophecy comes immediately after the humiliation of chapter 5:1. But it also means that out of the rubble of the kingdom of David a better, greater, eternal ruler will come. That ruler will deliver and save Israel (and us) from sin and death.

HIS BIRTHPLACE

The text addresses the little town of Bethlehem. There were two towns called Bethlehem in Canaan, but Micah specifies Bethlehem-Ephratah in the territory of Judah ("among the thousands of Judah").

Bethlehem-Ephratah or Bethlehem-Judah has a long history in the Old Testament. It is first mentioned in Genesis 35:19 as the burial place of Rachel, Jacob's wife. Later, during the period of the judges, it features as the place where Ruth, Naomi, and Boaz lived. Later still, Bethlehem is named as the birthplace of David. Much later, Bethlehem is named among the list of returning captives: Ezra 2:21 reports that 123 men returned from Babylon to Bethlehem.

The other Bethlehem is Bethlehem-Zebulun, mentioned in Joshua 19:15 as a city apportioned to the tribe of Zebulun. Bethlehem-Zebulun was, in fact, in the region of Galilee, and even more interesting, Nazareth was very close to Bethlehem-Zebulun but far away from Bethlehem-Ephratah. We might expect, therefore, that if Mary is from Nazareth it would be much more likely for her to give birth in Bethlehem-Zebulun instead of Bethlehem-Judah. But God had a different purpose for Mary and for Jesus Christ.

About Bethlehem-Ephratah Micah writes that it is "little."

The idea is not that Bethlehem was small in population, although it probably was, but that it was small in strength, inferior in social status, and insignificant in importance. We might be surprised at this. If Bethlehem-Judah was the burial place of Rachel, Jacob's favorite wife, and the home of Boaz and Ruth, and the birthplace of David himself, would that not have made it an important place? However, there is no evidence that the Jews ever attached any great importance to Bethlehem. David never exalted it or honored it as a royal city, and it lay almost unnoticed. Even its name, *Bethlehem* ("house of bread") and *Ephratah* ("fruitful"), did not bring it any honor in Israel. Bethlehem was overlooked, forgotten, ignored, even despised.

Moreover, Micah underlines Bethlehem's unimportance and insignificance by adding "little among the thousands of Judah." Literally, the Hebrew reads, "little to be among the thousands," that is, "too little to be among the thousands." That means that Bethlehem-Ephratah was too small, too insignificant, and too unimportant to be mentioned. In the book of Joshua, we find lists of the cities apportioned to various tribes. The book of Joshua lists over one hundred cities by name in chapter 15. Bethlehem is not mentioned there. The "thousands" of our text refers to the Hebrew practice of dividing the population into groups of one thousand for military purposes (Ex. 18:21; Num. 31:5). Bethlehem-Judah did not make that list either. All this is contrasted with the other Bethlehem in Zebulun. It did make the list in Joshua 19.

Micah teaches us that the Messiah, according to the flesh, will have humble origins, a very unimpressive beginning, and will be born in a very insignificant place.

First, he tells us that the Messiah will be born when the line of David is brought low. Micah 5:1 tells us that the judge (or king) of Israel will be humiliated and Zion (Jerusalem) will be besieged, but from there Micah moves to a humble town or village called Bethlehem. Bethlehem tells God's people that David's line shall be preserved. Every Jew knew that Bethlehem-Ephratah was the humble beginning of David himself. But Bethlehem also tells God's people that David's line will no longer flourish in Jerusalem: to receive the Messiah, David will have to return, as it were, to his humble roots. That is why these words, "But thou, Bethlehem-Ephratah," are both a message of hope (God has not forgotten his people) and a message of judgment (God will humble his people before he exalts them again).

Here Micah is echoing 1 Samuel 16. In that chapter, God sent Samuel to "Jesse the Bethlehemite: for I have provided me a king among his sons" (v. 1). When God rejected the older sons of Jesse, Samuel asked, "Are here all thy children?" and Jesse answered, "There remaineth yet the youngest, and, behold, he keepeth the sheep" (v. 11). Just as in Bethlehem God provided for himself a king of humble origins, the youngest and most insignificant of Jesse's sons, so God will provide for himself a king from Bethlehem again. The wonders of God's providence!

Second, Micah tells us that the Messiah will have a very lowly beginning, which is a common feature of messianic prophecy. When the Messiah is born, he will not be in a rich palace with all the trappings of royalty. Instead, the promised ruler will not even look like a king. The one born in the backwoods of Bethlehem is he "that is to be ruler in Israel" (Mic. 5:2), but his rule in Israel will have a very unimpressive, insignificant beginning. Who would expect a king to be born in Bethlehem and then to grow up in Nazareth, another despised place? Surely God's ways are not our ways.

This theme of a lowly beginning for the Messiah is repeated in other prophecies. Isaiah 11:1 speaks of a "rod out of the stem of Jesse, and a Branch shall grow out of his roots." Isaiah 53:2

proclaims a "root out of a dry ground" that "hath no form nor comeliness." Zechariah 6:12 prophesies that the Messiah shall be "the man whose name is The BRANCH," where the meaning of the word translated "branch" is "twig or sprout."

God arranged this in his providence deliberately for our salvation. The Messiah's lowly birth in Bethlehem is part of the humiliation of the Son of God, part of his suffering. Why does the Messiah choose to be born in the obscure village of Bethlehem instead of the royal city of Jerusalem? Why does he choose for his earthly parents a poor Jewish couple? Why does he choose for his nursery a stable and for his crib a manger?

The answer is that Christ was born in Bethlehem because we are sinners. That is a sign to us of the depth of our sin, and we must be humbled that the Son of God was so degraded and humiliated as to be born in Bethlehem. Christ's sufferings in Bethlehem culminated in the cross, where he suffered the full burden of the wrath of God for our sins. We must see Bethlehem-Ephratah in Judah under the shadow of the cross.

HIS ETERNITY

Nevertheless, if we think that the origin of the Messiah is Bethlehem, we are mistaken. In fact, the Messiah, strictly speaking, does not have an origin, for he is eternal. Micah 5:2 is not speaking only of the Messiah's birthplace according to the flesh. Behind his incarnation and his lowly birth are what Micah calls Messiah's eternal "goings forth."

The phrase "from of old" is used elsewhere in scripture, and it means not only a long time ago, but refers to eternity itself: "The eternal God is thy refuge, and underneath are the everlasting arms" (Deut. 33:27). "For God is my King of old, working salvation in the midst" (Ps. 74:12). "From everlasting to everlasting, thou art God" (90:2). "Thy throne is established of old: thou art from everlasting" (93:2). "Art thou not from everlasting, O LORD my God?" (Hab. 1:12).

The phrase "from everlasting" means literally "from days of eternity" and is a very strong expression of eternality. Micah does not teach merely that the Messiah has a very long family tree or that his lineage stretches all the way back to David. He is teaching that the Messiah is eternal, and therefore that the Messiah is God. The savior promised by God through the prophet Micah is an eternal, divine savior, the Son of God, our Lord Jesus Christ, as the New Testament scriptures abundantly teach us. If Micah were teaching here that the Messiah will come from David's line, he would be telling us nothing new and nothing particularly remarkable. But a savior who is eternal, a savior who is God, is the savior we need. We need a savior who has almighty power, because only Almighty God can deliver us from the power of sin and death. This text promises exactly that kind of savior. Therefore, such a text as this should be of great comfort to us.

Moreover, we need to examine the words "goings forth." Micah does not merely teach that the Messiah is eternal (as eternal as God himself), but he writes about the Messiah's goings forth ("whose goings forth have been of old, from everlasting"). A going forth refers to the place, the time, the mode, or the act of going out. In other words, the Messiah's goings forth refer to his activity.

We see this as we compare other examples of the word translated "goings forth." In Daniel 9:25 there is the "going forth" of a decree to build the city of Jerusalem. In Deuteronomy 8:3 there is the proceeding (going forth) of a word out of the mouth of God. In 2 Samuel 3:25 there is the "going out" (going forth) of David to do something. We learn from this that the activity of the Messiah is constant and eternal: there are "goings forth" (plural), and these goings forth are "from of old, from everlasting."

This is a reference to the truth that the Son is eternally begotten of the Father within the being of God, which truth theologians call the eternal generation of the Son. This refers to the eternal works of the Son: the eternal procession of the Holy Spirit from the Father and the Son and the eternal decree of election and reprobation. This is also a reference to the works of the Son in time. His first work was his work of creation in which he, as the eternal Word, spoke and brought all things into being. His work includes all his works of providence and all the goings forth of the Messiah in the Old Testament (as the angel of the Lord).

Therefore, God underlines here an eternally prepared and promised salvation. Our deliverance from sin and misery is no afterthought, for the Messiah who is decreed and promised is from eternity, and from the beginning this Messiah has been active in history, preparing by his many goings forth for his own coming to save his people. We can surely trust in such a God.

Although the prophecy seemed incongruous, the Messiah came exactly as Micah prophesied. When Israel and Judah were in captivity, God did not forget this promise, for he brought his people back to the land of Israel after seventy years, and he preserved Bethlehem as a city or town for many centuries. When it appeared that Jesus would surely be born in Nazareth, God caused a great political upheaval to bring Mary and Joseph to Bethlehem. God was always sovereign in bringing about the fulfillment of his promises. Moreover, Christ "goes forth" throughout the New Testament age as he gathers, defends, and preserves his church, and his "goings forth" will culminate when he comes forth as the judge of the living and the dead.

Sadly, several modern versions of the Bible obscure the beautiful truth of Micah 5:2. Consider the following renderings of the text:

But you, Bethlehem, David's country,
the runt of the litter—
From you will come the leader
who will shepherd-rule Israel.
He'll be no upstart, no pretender.
His family tree is ancient and distinguished.
(The Message)

"But you, Bethlehem Ephrathah,
though you are small among the clans of Judah,
out of you will come for me
one who will be ruler over Israel,
whose origins are from of old,
from ancient times." (New International Version)

The LORD says, "Bethlehem Ephrathah, you are one of
the smallest towns in Judah, but out of you I will bring
a ruler for Israel, whose family line goes back to ancient
times." (Good News Translation)

But you, O Bethlehem Ephrathah,
who are too little to be among the clans of Judah,
from you shall come forth for me
one who is to be ruler in Israel,
whose coming forth is from of old,
from ancient days. (English Standard Version)

These are inexcusable mistranslations, which serve only to
obscure the truth that Jesus the Messiah is eternal and therefore
God.

HIS RULE

The text tells us that the Messiah will be a "ruler in Israel." First,
this means that the Messiah will be the Messiah for the Jews. It was

to the Jews that God first promised a savior. The Jews had come to expect one who would come from the line of Judah and of David. That Messiah would deliver them from their enemies and especially from sin. That Messiah is the Lord Jesus Christ, who even today sits on David's throne. About Jesus the angel Gabriel said, "He shall be great, and shall be called the Son of the Highest: and the Lord God shall give unto him the throne of his father David" (Luke 1:32). On the day of Pentecost, Peter declared concerning Jesus,

30. Therefore being a prophet, and knowing that God had sworn with an oath to him, that of the fruit of his loins, according to the flesh, he would raise up Christ to sit on his throne;
31. He seeing this before spake of the resurrection of Christ, that his soul was not left in hell, neither his flesh did see corruption.
32. This Jesus hath God raised up, whereof we all are witnesses.
33. Therefore being by the right hand of God exalted, and having received of the Father the promise of the Holy Ghost, he hath shed forth this, which ye now see and hear. (Acts 2:30–33)

This does not mean that Jesus will be a merely Jewish king over an Israelite nation. Micah 5:3 tells us that when he is born, "the remnant of his brethren shall return unto the children of Israel," and verse 4 declares, "Now shall he be great unto the ends of the earth."

The New Testament teaches us that the children of Abraham and of Israel are all who believe in Jesus Christ, whether ethnically Jew or Gentile (see Gal. 3:29). Moreover, the brethren of Jesus are his people for whom he became flesh and for whom he died on the cross to redeem them from the devil:

11. For both he that sanctifieth and they who are sanctified are all of one: for which cause he is not ashamed to call them brethren,

12. Saying, I will declare thy name unto my brethren, in the midst of the church will I sing praise unto thee.

13. And again, I will put my trust in him. And again, Behold I and the children which God hath given me.

14. Forasmuch then as the children are partakers of flesh and blood, he also himself likewise took part of the same; that through death he might destroy him that had the power of death, that is, the devil;

15. And deliver them who through fear of death were all their lifetime subject to bondage.

16. For verily he took not on him the nature of angels; but he took on him the seed of Abraham. (Heb. 2:11–16)

Second, the Messiah will be the ruler for God himself. You see that in the text in that significant phrase "unto me." The Messiah does not belong to Israel or to you or me. We often say that Jesus is my savior, but really what we must say is that Jesus is *God's* savior.

This does not mean, of course, that Jesus saves, delivers, or rules over God. It means that Jesus comes in the decree of God, to serve God, to reveal God, and to glorify God. That was always Jesus' own confession: "I came down from heaven, not to do mine own will, but the will of him that sent me" (John 6:38). Again we are reminded of Jehovah's words concerning David in 1 Samuel 16:1: "I have provided *me* a king among his [Jesse's] sons" (emphasis added). God was never at a loss: who will the king be, where will the king come from, or where can I find a king? God's king was ordained in eternity, prepared throughout the Old Testament, and finally revealed and given in the New Testament.

Jesus, the Messiah from Bethlehem-Judah, rules by delivering his people from sin and death. The rest of chapter 5 will describe in some detail the rule of the Messiah. He will be a shepherd who delivers and then preserves his people.

Jesus Christ will save his people by the incarnation. That will be his great "going forth." He will become a man with our nature born in Bethlehem. He will redeem us by his death on the cross. For that very reason he will be born into this world. If sinners are to be saved and delivered, the Messiah must die. Furthermore, he will accomplish our salvation by his glorious resurrection, for death will not be the end of the one whose goings forth are from everlasting.

Those who are saved by this Messiah recognize and confess their sins, sins that made it necessary for the eternal Son of God to be born in humiliation. Not only do we recognize and confess our sins, we are sorry for our sins. Not only are we sorry for our sins, we turn from our sins in repentance and embrace by faith the Messiah, Jesus Christ, who died for sinners such as us.

If Jesus has come forth to rule over you, your life will reflect that. Jesus does not rule over us with a rod of iron and smash us into pieces like a potter's vessel. That is how he rules over the wicked (Ps. 2:9). Jesus rules us by his word and Holy Spirit, and he subdues our hearts to himself. The result is that we will no longer live as we please, making our own rules, living as the world does, but we will live in devotion to him. That rule of Jesus occurs in the church where the word is preached, believed, obeyed, and lived.

If Jesus is your king, you will love him. If Jesus is your king, you will obey him. If Jesus is your king, you will serve him. That is the blessedness of life in the kingdom of the ruler from Bethlehem-Ephratah-Judah.

Chapter 11

The Messianic Kingdom of Bethlehem's Ruler

4. And he shall stand and feed in the strength of the Lord, in the majesty of the name of the Lord his God; and they shall abide: for now shall he be great unto the ends of the earth.

5. And this man shall be the peace, when the Assyrian shall come into our land: and when he shall tread in our palaces, then shall we raise against him seven shepherds, and eight principal men.

6. And they shall waste the land of Assyria with the sword, and the land of Nimrod in the entrances thereof: thus shall he deliver us from the Assyrian, when he cometh into our land, and when he treadeth within our borders.

7. And the remnant of Jacob shall be in the midst of many people as a dew from the Lord, as the showers upon the grass, that tarrieth not for man, nor waiteth for the sons of men.

8. And the remnant of Jacob shall be among the Gentiles in the midst of many people as a lion among the beasts of the forest, as a young lion among the flocks

of sheep: who, if he go through, both treadeth down, and teareth in pieces, and none can deliver.

9. Thine hand shall be lifted up upon thine adversaries, and all thine enemies shall be cut off.

10. And it shall come to pass in that day, saith the Lord, that I will cut off thy horses out of the midst of thee, and I will destroy thy chariots:

11. And I will cut off the cities of thy land, and throw down all thy strong holds:

12. And I will cut off witchcrafts out of thine hand; and thou shalt have no more soothsayers:

13. Thy graven images also will I cut off, and thy standing images out of the midst of thee; and thou shalt no more worship the work of thine hands.

14. And I will pluck up thy groves out of the midst of thee: so will I destroy thy cities.

15. And I will execute vengeance in anger and fury upon the heathen, such as they have not heard. (Micah 5:4–15)

In chapter 5:2, Micah prophesied the coming of Jesus Christ from Bethlehem. The backdrop of this prophecy was great distress for the people of God. Before verse 2 can be fulfilled, God will give his people up into the hands of their enemies for some seven hundred years. Babylon, Persia, Greece, and Rome in turn will oppress the people of God.

Chapter 5 describes the kingdom of the Messiah and gives us a glimpse of Jesus Christ. But Micah does not describe that kingdom using language familiar to us, so there must be a fair amount of unpacking of the language before we understand it in our modern context. Micah prophesies of a shepherd-ruler protecting his people, who dwell as a triumphant remnant among the nations.

MESSIAH'S RULE

The first thing we should notice is that Micah describes the messianic kingdom using Old Testament terminology. We took note of that in our consideration of chapter 4, and we saw that this was normal practice for the prophets. In that chapter, Micah described the kingdom of Messiah as the exaltation of Mount Zion. In the Old Testament, the kingdom of Messiah could not be understood without Mount Zion. Therefore, the prophets used terminology familiar to their original audience.

The vision of Micah 5 complements the vision of Micah 4, in which chapter Jehovah promised the prominence of Zion in terms of geographical and geological supremacy. All the nations shall flow to Jerusalem to learn God's law, and the Messiah shall create peace among the nations, so that the nations shall no longer learn war, and God's people will sit securely under their own vines and fig trees. That promise means that in the New Testament age God will reconcile to himself Jews and Gentiles and gather them into one church, where they will enjoy peace with him through the forgiveness of sins in the blood of Jesus Christ.

In Micah 5 Jehovah promises peace in terms of the Messiah suppressing his people's enemies and preserving his people as a victorious remnant among the nations. We must not have the impression from Micah 4 that there will be no enemies of the New Testament church. Enemies will be present, but Christ will protect us from them.

Verses 3–4 make clear that Micah is describing the rule of Messiah after he is born in Bethlehem. Thus the standing and feeding of verse 4 will take place after Christ is born, and this activity is really taking place today throughout the New Testament age. The "peace" and "seven shepherds, and eight principal men" of verse 5, the wasting of "the land of Assyria with the sword" of verse 6, and the "remnant of Jacob" as the "dew" and "as a lion" of verses 7–8 all refer to the period of the New Testament rule of Jesus Christ.

Therefore, to understand this passage we must not be tempted by a literal interpretation or even push this all into some future millennial kingdom on earth. That would violate the basic rules of exegesis and make these verses irrelevant to us. Nevertheless, that does not mean that Micah had nothing important to say to his own countrymen and contemporaries. Like many prophecies, this prophecy has multiple layers of meaning and fulfillment.

In other words, if we claim that everything in Micah 5 refers exclusively to the New Testament age, the text has no relevance to Micah's contemporaries, which would make Micah a mocker of the people rather than a prophet who brings God's word. Messiah ruled in the Old Testament also, for his goings forth "have been from of old, from everlasting" (v. 2). But what Messiah does in Micah's day and throughout the Old Testament is only typical of and preparatory to what Messiah will do when he finally comes in his incarnation, death, resurrection, and ascension. For example, Assyria will be subdued in Micah's day (remember what the angel of Jehovah did to the Assyrian army in 2 Kings 19:35, when the Assyrians besieged Jerusalem during the reign of Hezekiah), but the real enemy of God's people will be defeated only when Messiah finally comes.

All that is necessary to understand the passage generally. What do we learn here, specifically, about the kingdom of Jesus Christ, a kingdom of which we are by grace the citizens?

First, we learn that the kingdom of Christ will endure forever. We see that in the words "he shall stand" and "they shall abide" (Mic. 5:4). About Messiah we learn that he shall stand, which is in stark contrast to the kingdoms of Israel and Judah. They shall fall, but Messiah shall stand because he is God's king—the king promised by God, and the king ordained and anointed by God. He shall stand "in the strength of the LORD, in the majesty of the name of the LORD his God" (v. 4). No enemy will be able to defeat, conquer, dethrone, or succeed Jesus Christ. That, for believers in Micah's day and for us, must be great comfort.

Because Messiah shall stand, Messiah's people shall abide (v. 4). The "they" of verse 4 are the "remnant of his brethren [who] return unto the children of Israel" (v. 3). We have already explained from Hebrews 2 and elsewhere that the brethren and children of the Messiah are the elect Jews and Gentiles who believe in Jesus Christ. The word *abide* in verse 4 is the same as *sit*: it refers to a peaceful, secure remaining without fear. Messiah will preserve his people in peace. No enemy, no matter how fierce and cruel, will be able to separate Messiah's people from himself. To use an example contemporary to Micah, the Assyrian, the cruel, wicked, idolatrous nation, the enemy of God and his people, will not prevail against Messiah or his people.

Second, we learn that the kingdom of Christ will be a universal kingdom. This does not mean that Christ will rule all nations in the sense that all peoples will willingly submit to him. When Christ ascended to heaven, he declared to his disciples, "All power is [has already been] given unto me in heaven and in earth" (Matt. 28:18). Although Christ might not always rule as we expect him to among the nations, over the natural creation, and over all the events of history, we must never forget that he has all power now and that he is ruling now. His rule has not in any sense been postponed. Nevertheless, we must not expect that one day all humans or even a majority of them will willingly worship the Lord. Even when only a small remnant worship Christ, we still maintain the truth that Christ's kingdom is universal and victorious.

Christ's kingdom is universal in this sense: he gathers and rules over a kingdom from all nations, not just one nation as was the case in the Old Testament. That is clear from Micah 5:4: "For now shall he be great unto the ends of the earth." His greatness consists in his standing and in the abiding of his people. That is also clear from verses 7–8: the remnant of Jacob will not be restricted to Israel, Judah, or Jerusalem, but will be "in the midst of many people[s]" and "among the Gentiles in the midst of many people[s]." That is an Old Testament prophet's way of saying, "In the New Testament age of the Messiah, God will save people from every nation under heaven." In chapter 4, Micah described the Gentiles flowing to Jerusalem; in chapter 5, Micah describes the church as an influence, a victorious and abiding remnant, among the nations.

Third, we learn that the Messiah will be a shepherd-king. We see that in the word *feed* in verse 4. That word means "to shepherd." To shepherd is a very particular kind of feeding: it is the feeding of sheep. Micah's audience was very familiar with the idea of the Messiah as the shepherd. They understood that Jehovah was their shepherd and they were his flock (Ps. 100:3).

The figure of a shepherd evokes in our minds a wonderful, familiar, and comforting image: a man, strong, resourceful, and wise, who loves and cares for his sheep. Although the Messiah will be severe against God's enemies, although he is possessed of the majesty of the name of Jehovah, and although he has the strength of God, *we* must not fear him, because he is not a tyrant but our shepherd. Jesus Christ is our shepherd, the Good Shepherd, who cares for us, provides for us, protects us, leads us, comforts us, and feeds us.

We are the sheep of Jesus Christ, who are helpless, foolish, and wayward and who need constant guidance and teaching. The shepherd feeds us by declaring to us the majesty of the name of God. We learn from the shepherd the greatness of God in all his works of creation, providence, judgment, and salvation. We are shepherded by Jesus through the preaching of the gospel as Christ sends pastors and teachers for the nourishment of his church. If Jesus is your shepherd, you will be found in the word, daily, and especially on the Lord's day.

MESSIAH'S PEOPLE

The first thing we learn about Messiah's people (the New Testament church) in this passage is that they are a victorious remnant.

Micah calls them "the remnant of Jacob" (Mic. 5:7–8), which is a term he uses elsewhere (2:12; 4:7; 5:3; 7:18). A remnant is that which is left over after a calamity destroys the majority. A remnant, by definition, is small in comparison to the whole of something. Micah promises the people that, although the majority will be destroyed in Babylon, God will not make a full end of his people. Because God is merciful and faithful to his people, he will keep his promise to save an elect remnant from the otherwise apostate nation.

Even in the New Testament when the remnant includes Jews and Gentiles from all nations, the church in history is never the majority but always remains a remnant. Nevertheless, God's people, whether in the Old Testament or in the New Testament, will be a victorious remnant.

Many look for victory and success, but they see victory almost exclusively in terms of numbers. If a majority is converted, if the church experiences revival, if the church controls political structures, then and only then is she thought to be victorious. But that is not how the Bible views and promises victory. In scripture, victory is measured by the fulfillment of God's purposes. If God purposes to save a remnant and succeeds in doing so, even if the remnant remains small, despised, and persecuted, that is true victory. When that small remnant is finally gathered into heaven and all the wicked are destroyed forever, God's victory (which was never in doubt) will be clear to all.

Paul describes this victory in Romans 8:36–39:

36. As it is written, For thy sake we are killed all the day long; we are accounted as sheep for the slaughter.
37. Nay, in all these things we are more than conquerors through him that loved us.
38. For I am persuaded, that neither death, nor life, nor angels, nor principalities, nor powers, nor things present, nor things to come,
39. Nor height, nor depth, nor any other creature, shall be able to separate us from the love of God, which is in Christ Jesus our Lord.

If your idea of victory does not include Christians being killed all the day long without being separated from the love of God, your idea of victory is carnal, not spiritual—worldly, not biblical.

The victory of the remnant is described in terms of victory over Assyria, which empire ceased to exist in the seventh century BC. Assyria stands for the enemy of God's people. In Micah's day the enemy *du jour* was Assyria, with its capital in Nineveh. Very shortly after Micah started prophesying, the northern kingdom of Israel with its capital of Samaria was captured by the Assyrians.

But Assyria ("the Assyrian" [Mic. 5:5]; "the land of Nimrod" [v. 6]) is representative of all the enemies of God's people throughout history. In Genesis 10–11 Nimrod is the king behind the tower of Babel, that ancient enemy of God's people and the first historical type of antichrist. In Isaiah 14:12 Assyria is really a picture of Satan himself. Therefore, Assyria stands for the spiritual enemies of God's people: sin, temptation, death, hell, the curse, the world, and the devil. Micah promises that the remnant, although small, will triumph over every Assyrian who tries to conquer her. In fact, the remnant will spoil Assyria and take her goods.

Micah 5:5 promises, "Then shall we raise against him seven shepherds, and eight principal men." Verse 6 adds, "They shall waste the land of Assyria with the sword, and the land of Nimrod in the entrances thereof." This means the church will prevail against the kingdom of darkness and even win converts from the wicked one and gather them into the people of God.

That curious expression "seven shepherds, and eight principal men [or princes]" requires some explanation (v. 5). Often the Bible uses such curious expressions with numbers: "These six things doth the LORD hate: yea, seven are an abomination unto him" (Prov. 6:16). "Thus saith the LORD; For three transgressions of Judah, and for four, I will not turn away the punishment thereof" (Amos 2:4). "Then shall we raise against him seven shepherds, and eight principal men" (Mic. 5:5). The idea is of going beyond a measure: six is the complete number, seven goes beyond; three is the limit of transgression, four is one beyond; seven is the perfect number of God's covenant, eight is one more than that.

The idea is that the church will have enough resources and more to repel the advances of the enemy and conquer in the power of Christ. The shepherds and princes refer to officebearers in the Old Testament and New Testament: whether prophets, priests, and kings, or ministers, elders, and deacons. We should include the office of believer as well. Never will God's church, as a victorious remnant, be lacking in spiritual supplies with which to fight the battle of faith.

The presence of the remnant among the nations has a twofold

effect, which Micah explains by using two additional illustrations: the dew and the lion.

In some countries, such as in Ireland, we do not think much of dew, because we have an abundance of rain. But Israel depended on dew for her very survival. During the months of April to October there was little rain, but every morning the ground was wet with dew. Dew is formed when water vapor in the air condenses at night and forms water droplets on the surface of the ground and on vegetation. It has a vivifying, refreshing, revitalizing effect.

In the Bible, dew is associated with God's blessing, and the withholding of dew is associated with God's chastisement or even God's curse. Isaac blessed Jacob with these words: "Therefore God give thee of the dew of heaven, and the fatness of the earth, and plenty of corn and wine" (Gen. 27:28). Haggai 1:10 declares, "Therefore the heaven over you is stayed from dew."

Dew is a fitting picture of God's blessing because of the way in which dew works. First, dew is heavenly: it comes down from heaven "from the LORD" (Mic. 5:7). Second, dew is pure: it is unmixed, unpolluted, distilled water from the air. Third, dew is gentle and works silently and without the intervention of man. Dew simply condenses at night, and there is nothing that man can do to produce dew or prevent dew: "that tarrieth not for man, nor waiteth for the sons of men" (v. 7).

How then does the remnant of Jacob (or the church in the New Testament) act as "dew from the LORD" and as "showers upon the grass"? We do so as a church by the doctrine that we bring, the health-giving, refreshing, vivifying doctrine of the gospel of God's grace that works by the power of the Holy Spirit. In Deuteronomy 32:2 Moses sings, "My doctrine shall drop as the rain, my speech shall distil as the dew, as the small rain upon the tender herb, and as the showers upon the grass." David sings about the blessings of Messiah's reign: "[Christ] shall come down like rain upon the mown grass: as showers that water the earth" (Ps. 72:6).

Thus by the preaching of the gospel, without much fanfare, the Holy Spirit, secretly, silently, and almost unnoticed, penetrates and influences the hearts of men. The same thing is true of the individual members of the church. We are, and must be, like the "dew from the LORD" (Mic. 5:7). By our witness, our godly example, our influence, and our prayers, we are a dew to refresh the world around us, to bring life to the parched souls of men. The Bible calls us "the savour of life unto life" (2 Cor. 2:16) and "the salt of the earth" (Matt. 5:13) and "the light of the world" (v. 14). To that we can add that we are the "dew from the Lord" and "the showers upon the grass" (Mic. 5:7). Are you refreshing in your witness or influence, or do you bring a drought to those around you?

There is another effect of the presence of the remnant of Jacob among the nations. This stands in sharp contrast to the dew. The remnant is like a lion (v. 8). Dew is refreshing and reviving; a lion is destructive and predatory. There is no more terrifying animal in the Bible than the lion: its fierceness is legendary, its roar is paralyzing, and its prey is helpless before it. That too is the figure the Spirit gives to Micah to explain to us the effect of the presence of God's remnant in the New Testament age.

This imagery is not unique or original to Micah. Jacob prophesied, "Judah is a lion's whelp: from the prey, my son, thou art gone up: he stooped down, he couched as a lion, and as an old lion; who shall rouse him up?" (Gen. 49:9). Later, Balaam prophesies, "Behold, the people shall rise up as a great lion, and lift up himself as a young lion: he shall not lie down until he eat of the prey, and drink the blood of the slain" (Num. 23:24).

These prophecies refer to Jesus, the Lion of Judah, and by

extension to his church. Micah promises that the remnant of Judah "treadeth down [tramples], and teareth in pieces, and none can deliver" (Mic. 5:8). This is true of Jesus himself: he trampled and tore in pieces all of God's enemies, especially the devil himself, when he conquered sin and death on the cross. This also refers to the church: the church is refreshing dew to some, but to others the church is the agent of their destruction, a marauding lion, a "savour of death unto death" (2 Cor. 2:16). Those who receive the gospel will be refreshed by it; those who reject the gospel will be destroyed by it. Either way, the church is a powerful force in the world not to be trifled with.

MESSIAH'S WORK

Messiah's work is, in the first place, to be the peace (Mic. 5:5). The Messiah is peace—our peace—through delivering us from our enemies. Peace is the absence of war, and especially here, peace is the absence of war because the enemies have been defeated. In chapter 4, peace was described in terms of reconciliation of the nations to God and to one another, as well as the enjoyment of the fruit of peace as every man dwelt under his own vine and fig tree. In chapter 5, peace is described in terms of deliverance from the Assyrian, who, as indicated earlier, is a type of all the enemies of God's people.

Notice how verses 5–6 describe this peace. First, when the Assyrian comes in, we, the church of Jesus Christ, shall raise up shepherds against him. Second, they shall waste Assyria with the sword. Third, "Thus shall he deliver us from the Assyrian" (v. 6). The peace that we enjoy (only because Christ has destroyed the Assyrian) is fellowship with God, in which God is in a harmonious relationship with us, blessing us and receiving us in love. That is only because Christ has conquered sin and death on the cross. Because we are sinners, we deserve that God be eternally at war with us. But God determined to reconcile us to himself by satisfying his own justice in the death of his Son. He paid for our sins. That is the peace. We see that in Ephesians 2:14: "For he is our peace, who hath made both one, and hath broken down the middle wall of partition between us."

The second part of Messiah's work is sanctification. We see that in the list of "I will cut off"; "I will destroy," in Micah 5:10–15. These can be arranged into two categories. First, there are the things in which Judah was tempted to place her trust, things not evil in themselves but hindrances to faith (horses, chariots, cities, strongholds). Second, there are the idolatries and superstitions that defile Judah as a nation and as a people (witchcrafts, soothsayers, graven images, standing images, groves: "Thou shalt no more worship the work of thine hands" [v. 13]). Judah as a nation was so addicted to these sins and vices that God promised in judgment to the wicked and in mercy to the elect to cut them off from her.

That, expressed in New Testament language, is sanctification. Christ makes us holy by cutting off our sins, not merely forgiving them but cutting them off. What are the things in which you are tempted to put your trust? What is the modern equivalent of a chariot or horse that you think you cannot live without? Christ in mercy, sometimes we think it is in harsh mercy, will take those things from us. What are the sins that defile you? Is it not encouraging to know that Christ will cleanse us of those things and will ultimately cut those sins from us so that we are devoted to him alone?

That too happens by the work of the cross. Listen to what Christ promises to do for us:

25. Christ also loved the church, and gave himself for it;
26. That he might sanctify and cleanse it with the washing of water by the word,

27. That he might present it to himself a glorious church, not having spot, or wrinkle, or any such thing; but that it should be holy and without blemish. (Eph. 5:25–27)

13. Looking for that blessed hope, and the glorious appearing of the great God and our Saviour Jesus Christ;

14. Who gave himself for us, that he might redeem us from all iniquity, and purify unto himself a peculiar people, zealous of good works. (Titus 2:13–14)

Let us, then, live in that hope, and let us submit ourselves to Bethlehem's shepherd-king and enjoy the blessings of his kingdom.

Chapter 12

Jehovah's Covenantal Controversy

1. Hear ye now what the Lord saith; Arise, contend thou before the mountains, and let the hills hear thy voice.

2. Hear ye, O mountains, the Lord's controversy, and ye strong foundations of the earth: for the Lord hath a controversy with his people, and he will plead with Israel.

3. O my people, what have I done unto thee? and wherein have I wearied thee? testify against me.

4. For I brought thee up out of the land of Egypt, and redeemed thee out of the house of servants; and I sent before thee Moses, Aaron, and Miriam.

5. O my people, remember now what Balak king of Moab consulted, and what Balaam the son of Beor answered him from Shittim unto Gilgal; that ye may know the righteousness of the Lord. (Micah 6:1–5)

In chapter 6, Micah returns to the present situation of Judah in c. 700 BC. In chapters 4–5, Micah had been speaking about the future. He described the peace and prosperity of the coming age of the Messiah. He did so using beautiful imagery and typology taken from the Old Testament realities familiar to the people of his day. He did so also against the dark backdrop of looming judgment and affliction.

But chapters 4–5 are a kind of interruption, designed to comfort the elect remnant. We must remember chapters 1–3, where Micah in Jehovah's name had indicted Israel and Judah (especially Jerusalem's leaders) for their sins. Micah is now reverting to that present reality: the people's sins must be exposed, and Micah is full of the Spirit of God to do that (3:8). Micah by the Holy Spirit uses every rhetorical device to impress upon the people the seriousness of their sins, but he is dealing with a spiritually deaf and stubborn nation.

At the beginning of chapter 6, Jehovah announces a covenantal lawsuit against his people. The language of our text is that of official court proceedings. Jehovah is the plaintiff, and Jehovah's people are the accused or the defendant. Micah is the prosecutor, the mountains are the witnesses and the jury, and Jehovah is the judge. Micah is called to "plead with Israel" (v. 2), which word does not mean to beg, but to indict or lay formal, legal charges against someone.

The charge against Judah is clear: unfaithfulness to God's covenant. Although the word *covenant* is not used here, the concept of covenant is clearly behind these words. Micah addresses the entire nation organically, as one living entity before him. He calls the entire nation "my people," which presupposes a relationship. The issue here is Jehovah's faithfulness, for Jehovah speaks as a wronged husband bringing his sinful, unfaithful, unthankful wife to court. "Look at what I have done for this people, and look at how they have repaid me!" Jehovah has the same controversy with the church today. We need, therefore, to sit up and take notice of these words.

JEHOVAH: THE FAITHFUL GOD

Before Micah reads out Jehovah's charges against the people and before Jehovah passes sentence, Jehovah protests his own innocence. This is a rhetorical device, of course, designed to underline Judah's guilt and to provoke her to shame. We might imagine a husband bringing his wife to court. He might say, in full assurance of his innocence, "Wife, testify against me. Wife, have I not faithfully lived with you for all these years? Have I not faithfully provided for you and the children? Have I not been faithful to my marriage vows? Wife, is there anything in my conduct that you can bring against me? Has there been cruelty, neglect, or unreasonableness in my actions?"

If a husband has been truly faithful, such a wife will have nothing to say. Her own conscience will accuse her. That is what Micah is doing in our text. He is prosecuting in Jehovah's name.

This is a rhetorical device because God never places himself in a position where we judge him. We are not competent to judge him: he is holy, spotlessly pure, unswervingly committed to righteousness; we are sinful, foolish, twisted, and perverse. We are inclined to judge things completely wrongly, contrary to truth. Besides that, we are without any power to enter into a controversy with God. No man can strive with the Almighty and prevail: "Woe unto him that striveth with his Maker! Let the potsherd strive with the potsherds of the earth. Shall the clay say to him that fashioneth it, What makest thou? or thy work, He hath no hands?" (Isa. 45:9).

Micah asks two questions in chapter 6:3 to bring out Jehovah's own faithfulness and to underline Judah's unfaithfulness. The first is: "What have I done unto thee?" (v. 3). The reference is to evil. Perhaps we can paraphrase Jehovah's opening statement this way:

What evil have I done to thee; what harm have I inflicted upon thee; what injustice have I perpetrated upon thee; how have I wronged thee; what unfaithfulness have I displayed toward thee? Judah and Jerusalem, my people, do you not live in the promised land; do you not have an abundance of blessings from my hand; have I not maintained you as my people for all these years; have you anything to complain about? When I have chastised you for your sins, can you ever complain that I have chastised you above what your sins deserved; is it not rather that I have not dealt with you according to your iniquities; is it not rather that you have wronged me?

The questions of verse 3 were designed as arrows to pierce Judah's collective conscience.

The second question is: "Wherein have I wearied thee?" (v. 3). To weary is to exhaust, to exasperate, or to frustrate someone. One might weary another person by placing excessive burdens upon him:

Have I made your life miserable and toilsome when I was your God? Is it wearisome for you, O Judah, to serve me? Is it a chore to pray to me, to offer sacrifices to me, to come to my temple; is it a bore to celebrate my feast days, to live in covenantal fellowship with me; is that boring, tiresome, wearisome, and bothersome? Is it wearisome to you, O Judah, to live in covenantal fellowship with your fellow saints? Is it a bore for you to love your neighbor and show kindness to him?

The truth of the matter is that Judah had wearied God by her sins and that Judah had wearied herself in chasing after other gods and in serving sin:

21. This people have I formed for myself; they shall shew forth my praise.
22. But thou hast not called upon me, O Jacob; but thou hast been weary of me, O Israel.
23. Thou hast not brought me the small cattle of thy burnt offerings; neither hast thou honoured me with thy sacrifices. I have not caused thee to serve with an offering, nor wearied thee with incense.
24. Thou hast bought me no sweet cane with money, neither hast thou filled me with the fat of thy sacrifices: but thou hast made me to serve with thy sins, thou hast wearied me with thine iniquities. (Isa. 43:21–24)

4. Take ye heed every one of his neighbour, and trust ye not in any brother: for every brother will utterly supplant, and every neighbour will walk with slanders.
5. And they will deceive every one his neighbour, and will not speak the truth: they have taught their tongue to speak lies, and weary themselves to commit iniquity. (Jer. 9:4–5)

Those same questions come to the church today and to us personally. Do you have a complaint against God that you want to raise today? Have you perhaps a bitter root in your heart against God? God says to you:

What have I done to you? Have I not given you the scriptures? Do I not give you the preaching as the chief means of grace? Do you not have the gift of prayer that you might commune with me? Do I not, moreover, give you your daily bread; and if I have afflicted you in my providence, can you complain that my hand is too heavy upon you? Will you dare raise a complaint against me?

Or do you perhaps find the worship of me wearisome, and do you perhaps prefer other things than to worship the God who made you and remade you after the image of his Son? Is it boring, tiresome, for you to listen to the preaching of the word twice every Lord's day; is the Bible a boring book to you; are my commandments grievous and burdensome? Do you think that I should have given you more, better things than he has given you? Are you thankful enough for the things that you already have?

Do not such questions shame us; are they not like sharp arrows in our conscience? They should be. We need to examine ourselves, lest God enter into a controversy with us.

Having protested his own innocence, Jehovah proves his own faithfulness, which Micah calls "the righteousness [literally, "the righteousnesses" or "righteous deeds," in the plural] of the LORD" (v. 5). In verses 4–5, Micah gives Judah a history lesson to remind her of God's great works of salvation.

First, Micah reminds Judah of the exodus from Egypt. Some seven hundred years prior to Micah's prophecy, Israel as a people did not exist, except as an enslaved, oppressed minority within the nation of Egypt. Israel had entered Egypt as seventy souls and over the space of four hundred years had grown to be a great multitude. In Exodus 2:23 we read, "The children of Israel sighed by reason of the bondage, and they cried, and their cry came up unto God." Israel had no possibility of delivering themselves; they were weak and powerless to escape the Egyptians, but "God heard their groaning, and God remembered his covenant with Abraham, with Isaac, and with Jacob" (v. 24). God in faithfulness to his promises delivered his people. He simply says in Micah 6:4, "I brought thee...out...and redeemed thee." Micah calls that great work of God "redemption."

To redeem is to deliver from bondage by the payment of a price. The price Jehovah paid was Egypt itself, for God declares in Isaiah 43:3, "For I am the LORD thy God, the Holy One of Israel, thy Saviour: I gave Egypt for thy ransom, Ethiopia and Seba for thee." Jehovah destroyed the Egyptians with ten terrible plagues in order to bring Israel to himself. Although that had happened seven hundred years before Micah preached, the inhabitants of Jerusalem still enjoyed the benefits of that redemption. They still lived in the promised land; they were still the free, redeemed people of God.

But they were not living as God's redeemed people. They were not showing by their actions that they belonged to Jehovah. On the contrary, by their actions they showed that they belonged to and wanted to belong to the world. Yet God calls them "my people."

Second, Micah reminds Judah of Jehovah's care in the wilderness. Jehovah never redeems a people to let them follow their own ways, just as a loving parent does not leave his children without supervision and guidance. Jehovah's goal in redemption is his own glory, and he is not glorified by children who run wild and free, living uncontrolled, ill-disciplined, and disobedient lives. Therefore, Micah adds, "I sent before thee Moses, Aaron and Miriam" (Mic. 6:4). Of all the events in the forty years in the wilderness, Micah mentions the leadership of Moses, Aaron, and Miriam, three outstanding saints of God: one the mediator of the old covenant and leader, one the high priest, and the third the prophetess.

This underlines the importance of good leadership and guidance. Where would Israel have been without Moses, Aaron, and Miriam, especially without Moses? Israel would never have made it anywhere near the promised land without them. Moses was the great miracle worker, the one through whom God provided the manna, the water, and the quails, and the one who received

God's word for the people. Miriam was a prophetess: she led the women in worship after the destruction of Pharaoh in the Red Sea (Ex. 15:20–21). Aaron, as the high priest, was indispensable for Israel. Without Aaron and his sons there could be no acceptable worship of God.

Third, Micah reminds Judah of Jehovah's protection from her enemies: "O my people, remember now" (Mic. 6:5). Of all the possible deliverances, Micah mentions Balak and Balaam from Numbers 22–24. Balak, the king of Moab, was afraid when he saw Israel encamped at the border of Canaan, in the plains of Moab, on the eastern side of the Jordan River, so he hired Balaam the prophet to curse God's people. Balaam was all too pleased to do this service for Balak, and the king promised to reward Balaam handsomely, but God prevented it. Three times Balak asked Balaam to curse Israel; three times (despite himself) Balaam was forced to bless Israel. Jehovah even declared through the mouth of Balaam, "Surely there is no enchantment against Jacob, neither is there any divination against Israel: according to this time it shall be said of Jacob and of Israel, What hath God wrought!" (Num. 23:23).

Micah urges Judah to remember what "Balaam the son of Beor answered" (Mic. 6:5). You can hear Jehovah: "My people, did not Balak and Balaam desire to curse you, but did I not compel him to bless you?"

What about the whole period of time from Shittim to Gilgal? Shittim was the last place where Israel camped before they entered Israel under Joshua's leadership. From there they sent out spies who lodged in Rahab's house; and from there they crossed the Jordan River by means of a miracle. Gilgal was the first camp after they crossed the Jordan: there the whole company was circumcised, there they kept the passover, and from there they conquered the land, beginning with Jericho. Therefore, from

Shittim to Gilgal includes the entire period from leaving the wilderness to entering the promised land. In all that time, Jehovah remained faithful to his people.

You can see from this the importance of Bible history. Some seven hundred years later, Jehovah expects his people to remember and be thankful for his mighty works. God still expects us to know this history and teach that history to our children: "We will not hide them from their children, shewing to the generation to come the praises of the LORD, and his strength, and his wonderful works that he hath done" (Ps. 78:4).

God has even greater works that he could mention to demonstrate his faithfulness to his church today. We therefore have even greater guilt if we live in ingratitude before him.

First, and most importantly, we live after the completed redemption at the cross. Israel enjoyed a typical redemption, redemption from Egyptian slavery. We enjoy the spiritual reality, redemption from sin. The devil is a worse taskmaster than the Egyptians ever were, and we had no possibility whatsoever of redeeming ourselves from his control. Our sins weighed heavily upon us, making us guilty before a holy God and worthy of his eternal wrath, and our iniquities were more than we could possibly count. Now because of Christ's work on the cross we are gloriously free to serve God.

Hear God in the gospel:

I have loved you with an everlasting love. I have chosen you to be my people. I have sent my Son, my only begotten, well-beloved Son. He lived and died, and suffered my wrath in your place, to pay for your sins; and I raised him to life again for your salvation. No price was too great to pay that I might have you for myself. Is all of that wearisome to you?

In addition, God gives us leadership and guidance in the church so that we may enjoy the redemption we have in Christ and be preserved in it. None of us would last a moment without the preserving grace of our God. We not only have the cross, which we view with great wonder and gratitude, but we also have the Holy Spirit in us, who enables us to live a new and holy life. We have the power of God's grace to endure temptation. God has not left us to our own devices to struggle to heaven in our own resources. We have at the end of a life lived in the grace of God the blessings of eternal life in heaven.

God calls us to remember his blessings "that ye may know the righteousness of the LORD" (Mic. 6:5). We could have used the word *mercy*, but Micah uses the word *righteousness*. God's saving acts are his righteousness, because in them God shows his faithfulness to all his promises. We do not deserve his salvation, but he has committed himself by an oath to give us salvation. John says something similar in 1 John 1:9: "If we confess our sins, he is *faithful and just* to forgive us our sins, and to cleanse us from all unrighteousness" (emphasis added).

Thus the question comes to us: In light of all that God has done for his people, in both the Old Testament and New Testament, how ought we to live? Do we have any excuse at all for a life of ingratitude and disobedience? Can we cite one example of unrighteousness in God? If Israel could not, even less can we.

ISRAEL: THE UNTHANKFUL PEOPLE

There is only one reason why Israel (and we) could not be moved by Micah's opening testimony from Jehovah God: ingratitude. When we live in disobedience to God's commandments, it is because we are unthankful. Israel had forgotten the great works of Jehovah. Very likely Israel no longer taught their children what

God had done in the exodus and how God had preserved his people in the wilderness. The names Moses, Aaron, and Miriam meant little to them. Redemption and deliverance from enemies no longer meant much to them: it was all such a long time ago (seven hundred years), and it made little difference in their lives. "Micah, preach something more interesting. Preach how God will give us wine and strong drink, and we will listen to that. But spare us a history lesson."

The same thing is true with the church today. Not only do many Christians today know almost nothing about God's great works, but few care to know. They know more about their favorite sports teams, the latest technological gadgets, the newest movies, the popular music charts, or the newest fads in fashion than they do about God's blessing of Israel through the prophet Balaam. If you mention these things, they yawn in boredom: "Who cares about that? That happened thousands of years ago! I want something more practical. What has God done for me recently?"

Even the cross has become boring for some Christians: it no longer thrills Christians to hear about Jesus Christ and him crucified. How do I know? The ministers of many churches do not preach him, and there is no demand to have him preached. If you do preach him, you will hear the cry that it is not relevant. We need, they say, to be relevant!

Micah underlines the stubbornness of the people by appealing to the mountains. In other words, because Judah will not hear, I Jehovah will shame them by having my prophet Micah preach before the mountains. The mountains are more responsive than this people called by my name! The mountains are witnesses, the strong foundations of the earth are the jury: they will hear the evidence presented by Jehovah against his people (Mic. 6:2). In chapter 1:2, Jehovah had called the peoples of the world to trial, and he declared that he would be a witness against them. Now in chapter 6:2, Jehovah calls the very creation to witness against Israel. This is fitting because the mountains were there from the beginning. The mountains were there before Israel, and they will remain when Israel goes into Babylon.

What a solemn occasion, then, is this. Jehovah as an aggrieved husband has Micah as prosecutor bring charges against Israel his unfaithful wife. Israel is arraigned, and she has nothing to say in her defense. God convinces her of her unfaithfulness and treachery.

The only hope Israel has is to repent and trust in the Messiah who will bear all her sins on the cross. Let us take to heart Jehovah's controversy, and let us remember that for us who believe, Jehovah's controversy was answered at Calvary. Let us who believe in Christ greatly rejoice and live in thankfulness before his face.

Chapter 13

Jehovah's Good Requirements

6. Wherewith shall I come before the Lord, and bow myself before the high God? shall I come before him with burnt offerings, with calves of a year old?

7. Will the Lord be pleased with thousands of rams, or with ten thousands of rivers of oil? shall I give my firstborn for my transgression, the fruit of my body for the sin of my soul?

8. He hath shewed thee, O man, what is good; and what doth the Lord require of thee, but to do justly, and to love mercy, and to walk humbly with thy God? (Micah 6:6–8)

In chapter 6, Micah, in the name of Jehovah, announces Jehovah's controversy with his people. In that controversy Jehovah cries out to his people: "O my people, what have I done unto thee?" (v. 3). Jehovah even declares: "Testify against me!" (v. 3). In so doing, Jehovah strongly protests his righteousness and the people's treachery. Then Jehovah proves from history that he has always been faithful to Judah. He brings as "Exhibit A" his deliverance of his people from Egypt, his sending them Moses, Aaron, and Miriam, and his protection of them in the wilderness.

Jehovah's "Exhibit A" to us is the cross of Jesus Christ. Surely, then, neither they nor we have any excuse for ingratitude toward God.

The text contains a kind of dialogue between the prosecution and the defense in Jehovah's controversy or lawsuit. Judah responds to Jehovah in verses 6–7. She shows in her response that she recognizes the majesty and holiness of God, for she speaks of him as "the high God" (v. 6) and she confesses sin: "my transgression…the sin of my soul" (v. 7). But her response to Jehovah is false: she does not know (or claims not to know) how she should approach God. Micah, in Jehovah's name, responds to Judah's question (whether it is a sincere question or not, or whether it is a question designed to escape blame or not). "He hath shewed thee, O man, what is good; and what doth the LORD require of thee" (v. 8).

JEHOVAH'S GOOD AND CLEAR REQUIREMENTS

Before we look at the three requirements, we need to ask and answer some questions. The first question is: what are these requirements generally? The text says two things about them: they are good, and they are clear.

First, they are good. "He hath shewed thee, O man, what is good" (v. 8). We are not interested here in what seems good to us, or even in what seems good to society. We are interested in what is good *to Jehovah*. Good in the Bible is defined by what is pleasing to God, not what is pleasing to us, and not what is pleasing to the greatest number of people. Because God is the good God, what is good and pleasing to him will also be good for us: it will be good for us spiritually and will bring us blessedness.

12. And now, Israel, what doth the Lord thy God require

of thee, but to fear the Lord thy God, to walk in all his ways, and to love him, and to serve the Lord thy God with all thy heart and with all thy soul,

13. To keep the commandments of the Lord, and his statutes, which I command thee this day for thy good? (Deut. 10:12–13)

Second, they are clear. "He hath shewed thee, O man" (Mic. 6:8). Jehovah is not a God who is impossible to serve because we do not know what he requires. He has shown us (each of us) what is good and what he requires. Jehovah has declared that to all of his people, not just to a select few. One does not require great insights, learning, or degrees in theology to know it. Jehovah's requirements are clearly recorded for us in scripture that we might know them. Our calling is to do these things in thankfulness to him.

The second question we need to ask is: for whom are these requirements, or from whom does God require them? The text explains that these are what God requires from us, his people. "He hath shewed thee...what doth the LORD require of thee... thy God" (v. 8). This text is not directed to the Philistines, the Moabites, or the Babylonians. It is directed to the people of God: "my people" (vv. 3, 5).

This text is therefore not directed to the modern society in which we live, for God does not call all the inhabitants of the world in general to live the Micah 6:8 life. That would be impossible. God calls the church (believers, Christians) to live this way. For one thing, how can unbelievers walk humbly with their God? The calling of an unbeliever is not Micah 6:8 but repent and believe in Jesus Christ. Only then will you be able to live according to these requirements.

"He hath shewed thee, O man" (v. 8). The text has a very

direct focus: Jehovah is not addressing the nation of Judah or the church of Christ as a whole in verse 8, but he is addressing each person individually and directly. This is not a corporate calling but an individual calling. It is not the calling of the church as a body to live the Micah 6:8 life, to do these things as part of her official work in the world. Rather, it is the calling of the individual child of God. It is not merely the minister's calling, the elder's calling, the deacon's calling, or the calling of the church as a body: it is your calling (and mine) to do justly, love mercy, and walk humbly with your God.

The third question is: why does Jehovah require these things of us? The reason God requires that we do justly, love mercy, and walk humbly with him is that these things are the way in which we show our gratitude to him. These three things are not radically new ideas that Micah invented, a new and trendy way of serving God, never tried before. These three things are a summary of God's law. These three things could be summed up by what Jesus said: "Thou shalt love the Lord thy God with all thy heart, and with all thy soul, and with all thy mind. This is the first and great commandment. And the second is like unto it, Thou shalt love thy neighbor as thyself" (Matt. 22:37–39). The reason we find these three requirements here is that Judah was not living this way: the people were living in oppression and cruelty and not living in close fellowship with God.

These three requirements, then, are not the three requirements for salvation. Micah is not offering a three-part "way to heaven" plan. Micah presupposes that the people who do justly, love mercy, and walk humbly with God are already believers. Salvation is not by these good works. If it were, none of us could be saved, because none of us does justly enough, loves mercy enough, or walks humbly enough to satisfy God. Rather, salvation comes to us by the unmerited favor or grace of God, who has adopted us to be his people and forgiven our sins in the blood of Christ. If you have that salvation, this is what God is seeking from you in response to him: a life of gratitude that consists in doing justly, loving mercy, and walking humbly with your God.

Given the answers to those three questions (What are these requirements generally; from whom does God require them; and why does he require them?), we can immediately rule out the most popular interpretation of this text for our day: social justice.

The "social justice" or "social gospel" movement is very popular among evangelicals today. The basic idea of the Christian social justice movement is that the church as an institution should be involved in ending injustice in society. The call from social justice churches is not to preach the gospel of Christ crucified, but to get out into the streets in order to make our city, our nation, and the world a better, fairer, more just, and more compassionate place. We must, urge the advocates of social justice, do justly by addressing income inequality, by campaigning for a higher minimum wage, and by campaigning for the rights of the disadvantaged in our communities. We must love mercy by helping the poor and homeless, by volunteering at the rape crisis center, by building hostels, hospitals, and schools in the third world, by bringing disadvantaged children to play sports, and so on.

That is not what Micah is saying here, and the Bible never teaches that such things are the calling of the church. If we think those activities and causes are the calling of the church, we will neglect the *real* calling of the church. The calling of the church as an institute and through her officebearers is to preach the gospel, to administer the sacraments, and to exercise church discipline. If an individual Christian wants to get involved in such humanitarian or altruistic activities, some of which are in themselves not wrong, he must understand that they are not the calling of the church as a body. The church in the New Testament never did these things. The charitable work of the churches in the New Testament was to collect alms for impoverished Christians.

Also it is very dangerous for the church to join hands with the ungodly to help make the world a better place. You cannot walk humbly with your God while you join hands with the wicked to help them in their causes. Remember the prophet's rebuke to Jehoshaphat: "Shouldest thou help the ungodly, and love them that hate the LORD? therefore is wrath upon thee from before the LORD" (2 Chron. 19:2).

Having looked at the three requirements generally, we look at the three requirements themselves.

The first good and clear requirement is "to do justly." The word translated "justly" is the Hebrew noun for *justice*. Justice in the Bible is to give someone what is his due under the law. In the Bible justice needs a standard. That standard is God's standard as revealed in God's law. That is one of the major problems with social justice. It makes no effort to discover what God's law determines justice to be. The idea of social justice is whatever seems just to man or to the greatest number of men. So, for example, today social justice is campaigning for homosexual rights or for reproductive justice for women (a euphemism for the evil of abortion). But justice is very simple: whatever God commands is good, and whatever God forbids is evil. All men must be judged equally by the law of God and rewarded or punished accordingly. That is justice.

We encountered this concept of justice or judgment in Micah 3:1 ("Is it not for you to know judgment?") and verse 9 ("Hear this...ye...that abhor judgment"). In Judah the people were defrauding, cheating, and stealing from their neighbors. They were living in blatant dishonesty and fraud. This was evil, and Micah condemned it very strongly. Christians must never be dishonest. But we must not think that biblical justice is that everyone has the same standard of living; we must not champion liberal political causes such as the redistribution of wealth or income equality.

Judgment is to treat your neighbor fairly and equitably, to give him what is right and proper. Do you do justly regarding your spouse, your parents, your children, your siblings, and your fellow church members? Apply the ten commandments, especially numbers five through ten. The Bible is not asking you to solve injustice in society, but God requires you to do justice in your own life, which is harder.

The second good and clear requirement is "to love mercy." Mercy is compassion, pity, or kindness. To love mercy is to delight to help those who are miserable by having compassion upon them. Mercy begins as an attitude, then it is a desire, and finally it blossoms into an act. Mercy must be something we love. We love to be kind, to be hospitable. We love to help others. We love to put the needs of others before our own. This mercy begins in our own families and is extended to our neighbors.

We must not misapply this commandment. It is not the calling of the church as a body or of the individual members to alleviate all misery and suffering in society. The church is not called to feed the poor, to help the homeless, or to promote government programs for social welfare. The church as a body does not have that calling. In fact, it is not part of the official ministry of the church to help the poor except through her diaconate, where she helps (primarily) her own poor. While the Christian does have a calling to help a needy neighbor, he does not have a moral obligation to support all charities that claim to help the needy.

The problem with government programs is that the

government takes the earnings of workers to pay for programs. The government never helps the poor with its own money.

In Judah there was no welfare program: the poor could avail themselves of the law (of gleaning, for example), but the law of God did not reward idleness and irresponsibility. The point, however, is clear: within Judah God called his people to have mercy on the weak and vulnerable, to alleviate the suffering of the needy, of widows, orphans, and strangers, and of the sick and the blind. We are called today to visit the sick, elderly, and lonely and to help the members of the congregation who need that help.

The third good and clear requirement is "to walk humbly with thy God." To walk with God is a beautiful expression of life in the covenant. The idea of walking with God is a daily, ongoing, moment-by-moment, constant living in communion and fellowship with God. One who walks with God knows God, loves God, delights in God, and lives for the glory of God. One who walks with God has his affections directed toward heaven and the things of God. Because two cannot walk together except they be agreed (Amos 3:3), one who walks with God walks in harmony with God, walking uprightly according to God's commandments. This walk, says Micah, is a humble walking with thy God.

Such a requirement rules out all forms of idolatry, which makes this requirement impossible for the unbeliever. Micah clearly does not mean that Jehovah requires each man to walk with the god of his choice so that the Philistine walks humbly with Dagon, the Ammonite walks humbly with Molech, and the Babylonian walks humbly with Bel. God is not pleased today when the Muslim walks with Allah, or the Hindu with Ganesh or Vishnu, for example. Micah means that Jehovah requires his people, who know him as their God, to walk with him.

That walk with God is humble. The Hebrew word for humble means "careful," so that the child of God never walks in a way that might offend God, never forgets the greatness and glory of God, and regulates his life to please God. Thus the believer, in walking humbly with God, walks against the world, loving righteousness and hating wickedness in all his works and ways.

In the midst of the social gospel movement very little is heard of this third requirement. Yet this one is fundamental and lies behind the other two. To walk humbly with thy God is simply a summary of the law: love the Lord thy God with thy whole heart, mind, soul, and strength. But social gospel or social justice tends to be at best ecumenical and syncretistic, and at worst atheistic and openly hostile to God. How can you walk humbly with your God while holding hands with those who are hell-bent on destroying morality and the family and promoting promiscuity, alternative lifestyles (sexual perversity), and the murder of unborn children? How can you walk humbly with God and with idolaters of all kinds? The more you walk with the wicked, even if the cause seems right, the more you will lose that close fellowship you ought to have with God.

God, then, does not require some great feat, some impossible work, but three simple things, which should be the way in which we are living anyway. Judah misconstrued what Jehovah wanted; she expected some great act of devotion, some extravagant worship practice, but Jehovah's requirements are clear, simple, and good.

Do not allow the social justice movement to burden you with false guilt: God does not require you to open a soup kitchen, end world poverty, find a cure for cancer, go on a mission trip, or renew the inner city. God requires of us the simple, everyday activities of doing justly, loving mercy, and walking humbly with our God.

By God's grace, we are doing that already. Especially the mothers are doing that regarding their children: parenting in the home is to do justly, love mercy, and walk humbly with your God. Of course, there are improvements we can make. Are those requirements unreasonable? Should God not expect obedience out of gratitude for what he has done for us?

THE HYPOCRITICAL RESPONSE

Judah responds to Jehovah's indictment in Micah 6:1–5 with religious hypocrisy. Judah asks in verse 6, "Wherewith [with what] shall I come before the LORD, and bow myself before the high God?" When the religious are indicted for their sins, their first recourse is more religion. They think that God can be pacified by religious devotion. The religious devotion that Judah offers is both extravagant and costly. She lists various offerings that she could make, each one more extravagant and costly than the former.

The offerings suggested in verses 6–7 are exaggerated. The first offering proposed is whole burnt offerings. Of all the offerings this was the costliest, because it was offered in its entirety to the Lord. The other offerings were eaten by the people and the priests in a fellowship meal, but the burnt offering was given only to God. Moreover, calves a year old were most valuable because a farmer had to care for the calf—feed it, prepare it, and provide for it—for a whole year before he offered it.

The second offering proposed is even more extravagant: thousands of rams and ten thousands of rivers of oil. If one ram is costly, how much more costly are not a thousand rams? Pure olive oil, which was offered with many of the sacrifices, was expensive. If a small amount of oil is costly, how much more extravagant would not thousands of rivers of oil be?

The third offering proposed is the costliest yet: "Shall I give my firstborn for my transgression, the fruit of my body for the sin of my soul?" (v. 7). Some of the Judeans, such as King Ahaz, had done just that. They thought they could please God with the supreme sacrifice, but in so doing they did something abominable.

Underlying these words in verses 6–7 is an implied accusation: Jehovah is unreasonable, impossible to please; nothing we offer is enough. A wicked accusation! But Jehovah did not demand such extravagant, costly worship, and God could not be appeased by such sacrifices if it all served as a hypocritical cover-up for sin.

That was the real issue: why did Judah want to appease God with worship? Because she did not want to be godly. Judah did not want to do justly, love mercy, and walk humbly with God. Judah wanted to do unjustly, hate mercy, love cruelty, and hate God. But she wanted to do it with a religious mask. She wanted to come to the temple and then defraud her neighbor, be cruel to widows and orphans, and live like the world throughout the week.

That is true with us as well. We think that if we simply go through the motions by coming twice or even once to worship on Sunday, we have satisfied God for another week, and we can live as we please throughout the week. John Calvin put it well: he said that hypocrites treat God like a child whom they hope to pacify with a toy or a rattle. That was Judah's attitude, and that is often our attitude too. At the end of Sunday or even after the second service on Sunday evening we say, "That is over for another week. Now back to what I really love."

God is not fooled by that worship. God's requirements are clear and good. He will not be fobbed off by hypocritical religious observances and activities. He demands our heart and life.

JEHOVAH'S MERCIFUL PROVISION

When Saul proved to be an unfaithful king, Jehovah provided

himself a faithful king, namely David. When Judah proved to be an unfaithful servant, Jehovah announced the coming of a faithful servant, namely Christ. We have seen throughout Micah that Christ is promised by way of contrast. Jehovah seeks a people who do justly; the people of Judah do unjustly and even abhor justice. Jehovah seeks a people who love mercy; the people of Judah live in oppression and cruelty. Jehovah seeks a people who walk humbly with him; the people of Judah walk in hypocrisy and mere formalistic worship.

Christ fulfills these three requirements perfectly. Jesus Christ did justly, for his whole life was in conformity to God's law. So much did he do justly that he bore the penalty of the law for us. Jesus Christ loved mercy, for he had compassion upon the sick, poor, and blind. He had mercy upon miserable sinners, and that mercy was displayed at the cross, where he paid for all our sins to deliver us from death and the curse. Jesus Christ walked humbly with his God. No one had greater communion and fellowship with God, and so much did he delight in God that he laid down his life to bring us into fellowship with God.

Do you struggle to do justly, love mercy, and walk humbly with your God? Jesus is not only our example, but he is also the source of the power we need to do that. Jesus gives us his Holy Spirit and grace in our hearts to live Micah 6:8. More than that, Jesus forgives us when we fall short of the life that Micah 6:8 sets forth.

Jehovah demands, Jehovah requires, Jehovah seeks, and Jehovah gives. Let us live this way, not to earn our salvation, not in our own strength, but in the strength of our God and in gratitude to him. That is the good way, the way of blessedness.

Chapter 14

Jehovah's Rod upon Judah's Marketplace

9. The Lord's voice crieth unto the city, and the man of wisdom shall see thy name: hear ye the rod, and who hath appointed it.

10. Are there yet the treasures of wickedness in the house of the wicked, and the scant measure that is abominable?

11. Shall I count them pure with the wicked balances, and with the bag of deceitful weights?

12. For the rich men thereof are full of violence, and the inhabitants thereof have spoken lies, and their tongue is deceitful in their mouth.

13. Therefore also will I make thee sick in smiting thee, in making thee desolate because of thy sins.

14. Thou shalt eat, but not be satisfied; and thy casting down shall be in the midst of thee; and thou shalt take hold, but shalt not deliver; and that which thou deliverest will I give up to the sword.

15. Thou shalt sow, but thou shalt not reap; thou shalt tread the olives, but thou shalt not anoint thee with oil; and sweet wine, but shalt not drink wine.

16. For the statutes of Omri are kept, and all the works of
the house of Ahab, and ye walk in their counsels; that
I should make thee a desolation, and the inhabitants
thereof an hissing: therefore ye shall bear the reproach
of my people. (Micah 6:9–16)

In chapter 3:8, Micah explained his commission from Jehovah: "But truly I am full of power by the Spirit of the LORD, and
of judgment, and of might, to declare unto Jacob his transgression, and to Israel his sin." Throughout the book Micah has been
unsparing in his denunciation of the people for their sins. In
chapter 1:5, he spoke of "the transgression of Jacob," which is her
rebellion. In chapter 2:1, he exposed the sins of rich landowners
who with violence seized the inheritance of their fellow Israelites
(v. 2) and oppressed widows and orphans (v. 9). In chapter 2:6, he
exposed the sins of the people for refusing to listen to the prophets and for preferring to be flattered by false prophets. In chapter
3:2, he exposed the people as butchers and cannibals, corrupt and
cruel, aided and abetted by the false prophets who prophesied for
money whatever their hearers wanted to hear.

Remember that Micah was preaching to the church of his
day. Micah addresses us. Have you rebelled against God? Have
you sought to enrich yourself at the expense of your fellow
church members? Have you faithfully and gladly heard God's
word, or have you murmured against it? Have you desired a flattering, ear-tickling, prosperity-peddling preacher? We know the
sins Micah denounces are prevalent in the church world today.

In chapter 6, after announcing God's covenantal controversy
and explaining to Judah Jehovah's good requirements, Micah
exposes the sins of Judah's marketplace. Jehovah required that
Judah love mercy, do justly, and walk humbly with him, but the
citizens of Judah lived in injustice and cruelty, and this came out

also in their business dealings. The sins of Micah 6 are commercial, that is, the sins of buying and selling, or the sins of doing business. Jehovah has a controversy with Judah here too: she is stealing from her neighbors in gross transgression of the law. Therefore, Micah announces coming judgment: a rod upon Judah's marketplace.

THE REASON FOR THE ROD

Micah brings us into the marketplace of Jerusalem some 2,700 years ago and into the houses of the rich men of Judah to show us what was happening there.

First, there was theft, sins against the eighth commandment. Imagine 2,700 years ago you are in the marketplace in Judah. You desire to buy a measure of wheat from a trader. Verse 10 identifies the "scant measure that is abominable." The scant measure is literally "a ephah of scantiness." An ephah was a measurement equivalent to about twenty-two liters or five gallons. If you wanted to buy an ephah of wheat, how could you know that you were buying a whole ephah? How could you know that you would receive your money's worth? You could not know. You had to take it on trust that the seller was giving you the correct amount.

In Micah's day, there was the "scant measure" (v. 10), that is, men were spending money on an ephah and getting less. In Amos 8:5–6 the prophet describes the same situation in the northern kingdom. This gives us further insight into the "scant measure." Amos 8:5 says that the traders longed for the end of the Sabbath so that they could make the ephah small and the shekel great. Verse 6 says that the traders looked forward to selling the "refuse of the wheat," that is, they would mix in with the wheat the dust and chaff from the threshing floor so that while the customer received a whole ephah in weight, he did not get a whole ephah of wheat in quality. For a poor person, who was living hand to mouth, to be cheated in that manner could be the difference between life and death.

In addition, there were in Micah 6:11 "the wicked balances" and "the bag of deceitful weights." This is a similar idea to "the scant measure." If a merchant had a set of scales or balances that were designed to give the wrong reading, he could easily cheat his customers. If a customer wanted to buy half a shekel of barley, and the vendor placed a stone on the scales that was actually only a quarter shekel, that vendor could charge the customer the price of half a shekel while giving only a quarter shekel. In Judah there was no one to check that the weights, balances, or measures were fair and correct. It was a matter of trust, and the temptation to steal was very great.

You might think that Jehovah would have very little interest in the buying and selling by his people, but Jehovah had made very clear in his law what he thought of such things:

35. Ye shall do no unrighteousness in judgment, in mete-yard, in weight, or in measure.

36. Just balances, just weights, a just ephah, and a just hin, shall ye have: I am the Lord your God, which brought you out of the land of Egypt. (Lev. 19:35–36)

13. Thou shalt not have in thy bag divers weights, a great and a small.

14. Thou shalt not have in thine house divers measures, a great and a small.

15. But thou shalt have a perfect and just weight, a perfect and just measure shalt thou have: that thy days may be lengthened in the land which the Lord thy God giveth thee. (Deut. 25:13–15)

A false balance is abomination to the LORD: but a just weight is his delight. (Prov. 11:1)

A just weight and balance are the LORD's: all the weights of the bag are his work. (16:11)

Divers weights, and divers measures, both of them are alike abomination to the LORD. (20:10)

Divers weights are an abomination unto the LORD; and a false balance is not good. (v. 23)

Second, there was deception or lying, sins against the ninth commandment. Three times, using three different Hebrew words, the text speaks of deception: "bag of deceitful weights" (Mic. 6:11), "the inhabitants thereof have spoken lies" (v. 12), "their tongue is deceitful in their mouth" (v. 12). In order to steal from someone, you have to be able to lie. Perhaps the merchants lied about the quality of their merchandise. Perhaps they lied about the origin of their goods. Perhaps the goods were counterfeit. Perhaps the buyers lied about how much money they had in order to get a lower price. The marketplace of Judah was full of lies, deception, and treachery by both buyers and sellers, and Jehovah was displeased.

The deceit was also used to cover up their crimes. It was connected to their violence. We have seen the sins of Judah's legal system in chapter 3: bribery and corruption necessitate lies. If an Israelite complained about being cheated, the solution was to lie, seek to cover up, and intimidate the complainant. If the complainant did not keep quiet, he was threatened with violence. There was intimidation. That is the third sin: "The rich men thereof are full of violence" (v. 12).

The source of this sin was idolatry, sins against the first and second commandments. Clearly, if a man worships another god than Jehovah, the God of truth, he will live in lies. This idolatry is implied in verse 16: "For the statutes of Omri are kept, and all the works of the house of Ahab." That must have been a shocking statement from Micah's mouth: Jerusalem and Judah, you keep the laws, commandments, and practices of Omri and Ahab. Omri and Ahab were the two worst kings in the history of the northern kingdom of Israel. They were, of course, long dead, but their evil lived on after their death.

> 25. But Omri wrought evil in the eyes of the Lord, and did worse than all that were before him.
> 26. For he walked in all the way of Jeroboam the son of Nebat, and in his sin wherewith he made Israel to sin, to provoke the Lord God of Israel to anger with their vanities. (1 Kings 16:25–26)

And Ahab the son of Omri did evil in the sight of the LORD above all that were before him. (v. 30).

And Ahab made a grove; and Ahab did more to provoke the LORD God of Israel to anger than all the kings of Israel that were before him. (v. 33)

It is scandalous that the men of Judah and Jerusalem did not walk in Jehovah's ways but in the ways of the worst of Israel's kings. We learn from this that when a man sins against the first table of the law, it leads inevitably to sins against the second table of the law. Love for the neighbor depends on love for God. Hatred for God drives out love for the neighbor.

We also learn that God does not accept the excuse offered today: "Oh, it is just business!" God watches how you do business and will judge accordingly. You must be sure of this: ill-gotten gains will not bring a blessing, for Micah 6:10 speaks of "treasures of wickedness in the house of the wicked" and says that the scant measure is abominable. The word *abominable* means the object of Jehovah's indignation or curse. God curses the dishonest businessman, the thief, and the fraudster.

Clearly, Micah is very relevant and up-to-date for us in the twenty-first century. There is still corruption in commerce in our day, and God still knows about it and judges it. We might be tempted to think that the primary application of this text is to the banking industry or big business, but we must remember that Micah is addressing the church. All the prophets address the church, not the world. The eighth commandment, especially here in Micah 6, therefore forbids commercial sins in the church.

When we buy and sell, we must be scrupulously honest. We must never sell something at a lower quality than the quality advertised. We must never sell something at an exorbitant cost. We must never try to squeeze the last cent out of our neighbor by tricking him. We must never use something without giving the proper cost of it. For example, a Christian may not ride the bus for free because he knows that the conductor will not check his ticket.

The Heidelberg Catechism Lord's Day 42 summarizes our calling under the eighth commandment:

Q. 110. What does God forbid in the eighth commandment?

A. Not only such theft and robbery as are punished by the magistrate, but God views as theft also all wicked tricks and devices whereby we seek to draw to ourselves our neighbor's goods, whether by force or with show of right, such as unjust weights, ells, measures, wares, coins, usury, or any means forbidden of God; so, moreover, all covetousness, and all useless waste of his gifts.

Q. 111. But what does God require of thee in this commandment?

A. That I further my neighbor's good where I can and may, deal with him as I would have others deal with me, and labor faithfully that I may be able to help the poor in their need.[1]

Do you treat your fellow church members and everyone with whom you live and work fairly and honestly? If you do not, your life is one of hypocrisy, and Micah calls you to be wise and hear the rod before you feel it.

In addition, we must apply this to the church in a different manner. There are times when the church is guilty of using wicked balances, deceitful weights, and the scant measure that is abominable.

The church does this when it dilutes and falsifies the doctrine of the Bible. There are many churches today where the measure is very scant, where the balance is wicked, and where the weights are deceitful. Men and women come to church expecting to be fed the finest of the wheat, but instead the minister gives a half-baked sermon where the word of God is not properly served. The Bible is falsified, twisted, and withheld from the church by wicked church leaders. This too is abominable.

Such wicked church leaders are the object of God's indignation and curse. Jehovah comes to many churches today and says, "Are there yet the treasures of wickedness in the house of the wicked, and the scant measure that is abominable?" (v. 10). Are there yet church leaders who have fleeced the people of God, who are living in luxury on the offerings of the people, and who have

---

1 Heidelberg Catechism Q&A 110–11, in Philip Schaff, ed., *The Creeds of Christendom with a History and Critical Notes*, 6th ed., 3 vols. (New York: Harper and Row, 1931; repr., Grand Rapids, MI: Baker Books, 2007), 3:347–48.

not fed the people of God with an equitable measure of food? Is there yet the trafficking of false doctrine and the merchandising of God's people by wicked and covetous men? What about the trafficking of relics and indulgences by the Roman Catholic Church? Listen to the sobering words of 2 Peter 2:3: "And through covetousness shall they with feigned words make merchandise of you: whose judgment now of a long time lingereth not, and their damnation slumbereth not."

THE JUDGMENTS OF THE ROD

Upon this thieving, lying, idolatrous people Jehovah threatens a rod. A rod is an instrument of discipline. Proverbs 29:15 says, "The rod and reproof give wisdom: but a child left to himself bringeth his mother to shame." When the reproof is not heeded, Jehovah takes out his rod. That is exactly what he promised to do in Psalm 89:30–32: "If his children forsake my law, and walk not in my judgments; if they break my statutes and keep not my commandments; then will I visit their transgression with the rod, and their iniquity with stripes."

Jehovah's rod is an instrument with which he chastises his people. Often Jehovah uses a variety of rods, depending on the situation and especially on the stubbornness of his people. Judah was ripe for the rod because she had not heeded the warnings of the prophets. The impenitence of Judah comes out in the question of Micah 6:10: "Are there yet...?" After all the warnings, all the sermons, and all the prophecies, are there *still...*?

The rod that Jehovah sends has a twofold effect and a twofold purpose. First, the rod destroys the wicked, reprobate majority of the nation. God's judgments always do that. Not everyone, not even most, of Judah were elect children of God, for many of them were wicked, unbelieving, and impenitent. Remember, "they are not all Israel, which are of Israel" (Rom. 9:6). Jehovah's rod would not reform them, but it would destroy them. Micah speaks of "smiting" (6:13); "making thee desolate" (v. 13); and "mak[ing] thee a desolation" and a "hissing" (v. 16).

Second, the rod chastens the elect remnant of the nation. They would not escape the rod, for they too would experience the rod, although it would not destroy them. The rod of correction is like the rod in the hand of a father who appoints the rod and tempers the blows with love. God lays only as many blows as are necessary to bring to repentance. Judah was a stubborn, rebellious child, defiant in her sins, so that she almost dared Jehovah to beat her: "Ye walk in their counsels; *that I should* make thee a desolation" (v. 16, emphasis added). The rod that Jehovah uses is the Assyrians and later the Babylonians. God uses such a wicked instrument in order to chastise his people: "O Assyrian, the rod of mine anger, and the staff in their hand is mine indignation" (Isa. 10:5). Micah does not describe Assyria as such. Rather, he describes the effect that the Assyrian and then the Babylonian invasion will have.

God's rod is first hunger, famine, sickness, and the sword. In Micah 6:13, God declares, "Therefore also will I make thee sick." The phrase *to make sick* means "to make weak, to bruise, or to wound someone with a heavy blow." The effect of Jehovah's beating will be devastation. Judah shall be desolate or made into a desert or a wasteland. The reference could be to a literal or physical sickness, such as a plague, or it could refer to a spiritual illness or affliction.

In verse 14, God declares, "Thy casting down shall be in the midst of thee." This word rendered "casting down" most likely means emptiness caused by hunger. Indeed, Judah's attempts to store up her ill-gotten gains or to preserve them from the enemy will be in vain: "Thou shalt take hold, but shalt not deliver; and that which thou deliverest will I give up to the sword" (v. 14).

Second, God will judge Judah with futility. Micah describes various activities of the people that shall be in vain because the people will not enjoy the fruits of their labor: sowing but not reaping (v. 15); eating but not being full (v. 14); treading olives but not using oil (v. 15); treading grapes but not drinking the wine (v. 15). God has a way of making all our effort come to nothing because the methods we used were sinful and dishonest. This is fitting because it is good that we do not enjoy the fruits of sin.

In a word, Micah threatens condemnation. That comes out in the rhetorical question in verse 11, "Shall I count them pure?" God will not count those pure and innocent who commit the sins described here. God will find out and punish every man for his iniquities. The result in verse 16 is "desolation," "hissing," or "reproach." Men will walk by Judah and Jerusalem one day and be horrified by their destruction. Men will hiss at Jerusalem. They will despise her, taunt her, and pour scorn upon her, and she shall be the object of men's jokes. That often happens when God chastises his people: so severe is God's chastisement that men stand back in horror and the wicked even deride the believer who has fallen.

Micah has sharp words of rebuke and judgment for Judah. Let us take them to heart. Let us hear the rod and who has appointed it. Better to hear it than to feel it!

THE HOPE OF THE ROD

This is a judgment oracle, and hope is not on the foreground, but there is hope. Micah addresses "the man of wisdom" and calls Judah "my people" (v. 16). If there were no hope, Micah would not even warn Judah, but Jehovah would simply destroy the nation without warning. But here "the LORD's voice crieth unto the city" (v. 9). Behold the longsuffering of our God! As wicked and apostate as she had become, God's beloved people were still there. If there were no hope, Micah would not speak of the man of wisdom (v. 9). There was still an elect remnant in the nation for whose sake God sent prophets: they would hear the rod and they would recognize their Father's hand.

Are you a man or a woman of wisdom? Do you recognize in your life and in the church the voice of God? You should because you hear that voice every week from the pulpit, and every time you open the scriptures you hear the voice of God.

Do you hear God's rod, or are you so foolish that you only hear it when it cracks upon your back? But even when God chastises you, he gives you space to repent:

5. And ye have forgotten the exhortation which speaketh unto you as unto children, My son, despise not thou the chastening of the Lord, nor faint when thou art rebuked of him:

6. For whom the Lord loveth he chasteneth, and scourgeth every son whom he receiveth.

7. If ye endure chastening, God dealeth with you as with sons; for what son is he whom the father chasteneth not?

8. But if ye be without chastisement, whereof all are partakers, then are ye bastards, and not sons.

9. Furthermore we have had fathers of our flesh which corrected us, and we gave them reverence: shall we not much rather be in subjection unto the Father of spirits, and live?

10. For they verily for a few days chastened us after their own pleasure; but he for our profit, that we might be partakers of his holiness.

11. Now no chastening for the present seemeth to be joyous, but grievous: nevertheless afterward it yieldeth

the peaceable fruit of righteousness unto them which are exercised thereby. (Heb. 12:5–11)

The hope for Judah and the hope for us is not in the rod, but in the one promised in the rest of this beautiful book: Jesus Christ will hear the rod and submit to it.

Christ will submit to the rod by humbling himself while the Father rains down blow upon blow, strike upon strike, wound upon wound upon his beloved Son:

Yet it pleased the LORD to bruise him; he hath put him to grief: when thou shalt make his soul an offering for sin, he shall see his seed, he shall prolong his days, and the pleasure of the LORD shall prosper in his hand. (Isa. 53:10)

He that spared not his own Son, but delivered him up for us all, how shall he not with him also freely give us all things? (Rom. 8:32)

Jesus Christ suffered the rod of Jehovah's anger so that we will only ever feel the rod of chastisement in the Father's love. The wicked, who are not his children, shall be beaten to destruction and dashed to pieces, but we, who are his children, will be corrected in measure. How then shall we live in response to that? Shall we live as Micah's contemporaries in dishonesty and theft? Shall we learn the ways of the heathen and walk in the ways of the false church? God forbid. Salvation demands a life of thankfulness, and that thankfulness is seen in our obedience.

Let us be wise. Let us heed the rod. And let us hear the voice of our God.

Chapter 15

Micah's Fruitless Search for Fellowship

1. Woe is me! for I am as when they have gathered the summer fruits, as the grapegleanings of the vintage: there is no cluster to eat: my soul desired the firstripe fruit.
2. The good man is perished out of the earth: and there is none upright among men: they all lie in wait for blood; they hunt every man his brother with a net.
3. That they may do evil with both hands earnestly, the prince asketh, and the judge asketh for a reward; and the great man, he uttereth his mischievous desire: so they wrap it up.
4. The best of them is as a brier: the most upright is sharper than a thorn hedge: the day of thy watchmen and thy visitation cometh; now shall be their perplexity.
5. Trust ye not in a friend, put ye not confidence in a guide: keep the doors of thy mouth from her that lieth in thy bosom.
6. For the son dishonoureth the father, the daughter riseth up against her mother, the daughter in law against her mother in law; a man's enemies are the men of his own house.

7. Therefore I will look unto the Lord; I will wait for the
   God of my salvation: my God will hear me. (Micah
   7:1–7)

Micah's final chapter is the elect remnant's response to the
first six chapters. Micah acts as their spokesman, putting into
words the thoughts of their hearts. There is evidence of repentance (Mic. 7:9), faith (vv. 7–9), hope (v. 14), and joy (vv. 18–20).
The Holy Spirit has worked through Micah's warnings and
promises to prick the hearts of some of the people of Judah. The
majority remain in their sins, but a remnant turns to God.

The first section of chapter 7 is a lament, beginning with
the words, "Woe is me!" (v. 1). The prophet gives voice to the
oppressed, faithful minority who are helpless to change the
direction of Judah. It is possible that Micah preached this during
the reign of King Ahaz. In that day, those who did justly, loved
mercy, and walked humbly with their God (6:8) were few and far
between. In this section we see the bitter fruits of apostasy from
Jehovah: departure from the covenantal God leads to a breakdown of covenantal life. A healthy covenantal life is impossible
without true devotion to God in the truth.

MICAH'S DESIRE

Micah's desire was for covenantal fellowship with his fellow saints,
whom he likens to the sweetness of the "firstripe fruit" (v. 1). The
covenant is friendship with God, blessed and happy communion
with Jehovah himself. Jehovah is the God of his people, whom he
has chosen and redeemed from sin and death. Jehovah's covenant
was revealed to Israel especially at Sinai, where Jehovah took his
newly redeemed people and constituted them a nation of priests
to himself. That covenant is even more clearly revealed in the New

Testament with the death and resurrection of Jesus Christ and the outpouring of the Holy Spirit. The covenant is confirmed in the blood of Jesus Christ, for by his death he removes our sin so that we can have fellowship with Jehovah our God.

The essence of true religion, therefore, is indeed a relationship, a relationship called the covenant, in which Jehovah is our God and we are his people. The covenant is a relationship of friendship in which we love God who first loved us. However, since the covenant is a relationship with the Almighty, it is not a friendship between equals. Our God *does* make demands of us. We have our part in the covenant, which is to live faithfully, obediently, and devotedly before him. We express our love for God by delighting to know him as he reveals himself in his word, worshiping him, communing with him in prayer, and obeying him.

But the covenant is never meant to be lived in isolation. Covenantal life with Jehovah requires and demands covenantal fellowship with other believers. The covenant is communal, not individualistic. In Micah's day the covenantal community was Judah; in our day the covenantal community is the church.

That covenantal life manifests itself in the various relationships that Micah mentions in the text. That Micah is disappointed by what he finds in Judah does not annul the truth that these relationships are supposed to be covenantal. Micah mentions three spheres: the immediate family, the wider family, and friends. To that we can add the general brotherhood of the nation of Judah. All of these relationships are (or ought to be) covenantal relationships where one can enjoy fellowship with fellow saints as a reflection of one's fellowship with God himself.

Let us mention, briefly, the different relationships in Micah 7. First, in verse 5, there is the relationship of friend. Friendship has three aspects: affection, knowledge, and sharing of life. Perhaps the best example of covenantal friendship is David and Jonathan in 1 Samuel 18:1: "And it came to pass, when he had made an end of speaking unto Saul, that the soul of Jonathan was knit with the soul of David, and Jonathan loved him as his own soul." Or consider the truth of Proverbs 18:24: "A man that hath friends must shew himself friendly: and there is a friend that sticketh closer than a brother."

Second, in verse 5, there is the relationship of a guide. A guide is a close friend with whom one is familiar, with whom one is united in intimacy, one in whom one would ordinarily confide and seek counsel (Ps. 55:13).

Third, in verse 5, there is the relationship of "her that lieth in thy bosom." Clearly, this is one's wife, one's closest friend. From a wife a husband must keep no secrets; with a wife there should be a full sharing of life and full, intimate love and trust.

Fourth, in verse 6, there is the relationship of other family members (sons, daughters, parents, in-laws, and members of one's own house). A covenantal home should be a place where love, fellowship, peace, and trust are enjoyed. To all of this we must add the truth that all Israelites or Judeans were brothers and sisters, and that today all Christians in the church are brethren called to live in fellowship together.

Micah uses an agricultural figure to describe his desire for fellowship: he likens himself to one whose soul desires "the firstripe fruit" (v. 1). The "firstripe fruit" is literally "the early fig." The fig tree in Israel yielded an early and a late crop of figs, one in June and the other in August. Of these two crops, the first ripe figs were the sweetest. The first ripe figs were especially prized because they were first, and they came after a long period from December to March when the fig trees were bare. You can imagine, therefore, the joy with which the Hebrews welcomed the first figs of early summer. Micah describes his great longing for such a succulent morsel in verse 1: "There is no cluster to eat: my soul desired the firstripe fruit." But of course Micah is using a simile: "I am *as when...*" (emphasis added). The first ripe fruit Micah seeks is the "good man" or "the upright" (v. 2).

The word *good* is a very distinctive word, for it can be translated as "godly," "faithful," "saint," "merciful," "kind," or "pious." The word has the same root as the word *mercy*: a good man is one who has experienced Jehovah's mercy and who exercises mercy to others. He does justly, loves mercy, and walks humbly with Jehovah his God (6:8). Elsewhere, Psalm 16:3 calls the saints "the excellent, in whom is all my delight." Micah earnestly sought the fellowship of such good and upright men in Judah: he wanted to enjoy the sweetness of their company; he longed to commune with them; he desired (as much as a man desires the first ripe fig of summer) to spend time with the saints. Micah's desire is expressive of the yearning of every child of God.

Remember Micah is not expressing merely his own thoughts on the matter. Micah is writing under inspiration on behalf of the godly remnant in the nation of Judah. Surrounded by the wicked majority, Micah and this godly remnant are famished for lack of sweet fellowship with the saints. Every Christian today must have the same desire: a desire for fellowship with godly family members, with godly friends, and with godly church members. The fellowship that draws Christians together is based not on similarities in age, social class, or nationality, but on a common salvation in Jesus Christ. All Christians have the same Father, the same Savior, the same Holy Spirit, the same salvation, and the same hope. Therefore, they desire to be with those with whom they share the deepest and sweetest aspect of their life.

There are some professing Christians who do not evidence much desire for this. If you invite them to church, to Bible study, or to other occasions where they can fellowship with God's people, they make excuses because they are not interested. In fact, they show by their priorities that they would much rather spend time with unbelievers. They are certainly not the kind of people who long for fellowship with God's people as men whose mouths long for the sweetness of the first ripe fig.

MICAH'S DISAPPOINTMENT

Micah looked for evidence of that covenantal life in Jerusalem and Judah where he prophesied, but Micah was sorely disappointed. He expresses the sorrow of the elect remnant: "Woe is me" (Mic. 7:1).

Let us return to Micah's field or vineyard in verse 1. Micah has gone there looking for a sweet morsel to satisfy his hunger. Micah is too late: summer is past and "they have gathered the summer fruits." Moreover, Micah is too late even to glean the leftovers from the field: "I am…as the grapegleanings of the vintage." This has two possible meanings: either Micah has come to the field after the gleaners have finished, or Micah is himself an isolated leftover grape that the grape gleaners have missed. Micah refers here to the Old Testament law of Deuteronomy 24:19–22:

19. When thou cuttest down thine harvest in thy field, and hast forgot a sheaf in the field, thou shalt not go again to fetch it: it shall be for the stranger, for the fatherless, and for the widow: that the Lord thy God may bless thee in all the work of thine hands.
20. When thou beatest thine olive tree, thou shalt not go over the boughs again: it shall be for the stranger, for the fatherless, and for the widow.
21. When thou gatherest the grapes of thy vineyard, thou shalt not glean it afterward: it shall be for the stranger, for the fatherless, and for the widow.

22. And thou shalt remember that thou wast a bondman in the land of Egypt: therefore I command thee to do this thing.

Micah is disappointed because there is no cluster to eat, for the harvesters and then the gleaners have picked the fields and vineyards bare. As indicated above, the summer fruit, the clusters, and the first ripe fruit refer to saints. "The good man is perished out of the earth" (Mic. 7:2). The men who do justly, love mercy, and walk humbly with God are gone. They have perished; they have died; they have probably been killed by the wicked. "There is none upright among men" (v. 2). There are no men who live in harmony with God's law and commandments. Micah does not mean that he alone is left who serves God, but that the righteous in Judah are so scarce that they are like a grape here and there, missed by the gleaners. They are not even enough to form a cluster, for their presence in Judah is almost negligible. Instead of good and upright men, Micah finds wickedness, cruelty, and treachery of the most shocking kind, which he describes in detail in verses 2–6.

First, the people are cruel (v. 2). Micah has already described the cruelty of the people using the metaphor of cannibalistic butchers in chapter 3. Now he uses the metaphor of a hunter. The men of Micah's day are so far from being good that they lie in wait for blood. They wait for an unsuspecting victim to pass by so that they can ensnare him in a net. They care not for mercy as long as they can bleed their brothers dry. Remember, Micah is not describing the heathen from whom cruelty is expected, but the covenantal community of Judah, whom he calls brothers. Sometimes professing Christians are crueler, fiercer, more cutting, and more hurtful than the wicked. My brethren, this ought not to be!

Second, the people are greedy and dishonest. Micah now uses the metaphor of a thorn hedge (vv. 3–4). A hedge is designed for protection: to keep enemies out and to keep sheep in safety. But a thorn hedge only tears, scratches, and wounds those who come into contact with it. The best of them, the really good people in Judah, are "as a brier." The most upright is "sharper than a thorn hedge" (v. 4). If that was a description of the best and most upright, what must the worst and most lawless have been like! The people of Micah's day were hard, harsh, sharp, cruel, and piercing, utterly devoid of kindness, mercy, and compassion. How about you: are your words sharp, cutting, designed to hurt rather than to heal and encourage? Do you lash out in impatient anger at others, or are your words and deeds sweet and refreshing? Verse 3 describes the people's dishonesty in business and in the law courts. In a word, corruption had spread to every walk of life.

Third, this wickedness had spread deep into families. Corruption, evil, and cruelty were not merely found in business and judicial life. The homes were filled with wickedness. A lack of love for God led to the breakdown of family life. There was no love between parents and children: "The son dishonoureth the father, the daughter riseth up against her mother" (v. 6). Love was absent among family members: "The daughter in law [riseth up] against her mother in law; a man's enemies are the men of his own house" (v. 6). Even friendships had broken down through lack of trust: "Trust ye not in a friend, put ye not confidence in a guide; keep the doors of thy mouth from her that lieth in thy bosom" (v. 5). What an awful thing when a believer cannot even fellowship with his closest family, cannot trust his closest friend, and cannot confide in his own spouse for fear of betrayal! Such is the case when the covenantal God is despised, and such is the case in times of persecution. Jesus refers to this passage in Matthew 10:34–36:

34. Think not that I am come to send peace on earth: I came not to send peace, but a sword.
35. For I am come to set a man at variance against his father, and the daughter against her mother, and the daughter in law against her mother in law.
36. And a man's foes shall be they of his own household.

This is a great pain borne by many in the church today.

Micah expresses his great disappointment in a lament: "Woe is me!" When a minority cannot change the situation, the calling is (at least) to lament. A lament is not the same as a bitter complaint against God, but is an expression of grief. Complaining, murmuring, or grumbling is sin, for it is a lack of contentment and a failure or refusal to trust in God. Grief is not sin: grief is the expression of anguish from a soul in sorrow or in pain. It was deeply painful for Micah to live in an apostate nation, commissioned to bring the message of God's judgment on a people whom he loved.

Micah's lament was perfectly justified and very understandable. He was right to go to the vineyard and expect to find a tasty morsel, a ripe fig, or a cluster of grapes to refresh his soul. Micah had been preaching for years, and he had every reason to expect fruit from his preaching, but instead of seeing a reformation he saw a worsening of the situation. He saw the people emboldened in wickedness. What a disappointment for the faithful prophet!

Micah had seen his preaching (for the most part) fall on deaf ears and hardened hearts. The people did not heed his warnings. They scoffed at him, they went on in their sins, and they even told him to be quiet. There is no greater grief for a preacher than to see those on whom he has expended the labor of preaching and teaching walk in sin.

Nevertheless, Micah does did not give up; he did not

become like Elijah, sit under the juniper tree, and request to die. He continued to preach. In chapter 7:4 he warns again: "The day of thy watchmen and thy visitation cometh; now shall be their perplexity." That day is the day of which he, the watchman in Zion, has warned, the day when Jehovah would visit Judah for her sins. They would see a foretaste of it with the Assyrian attack in Hezekiah's day, and the end would come when Babylon invaded.

That is our calling when the church is apostate and true Christians are few and far between: to lament before God and to seek out fellowship in the truth wherever it can be found. Micah did not adopt the attitude of many: "If you cannot beat them, join them. The wicked will not change, so I might as well join them in their wickedness. My unbelieving friends will never come with me to church or Bible study, so I might as well go with them to the nightclub or get drunk with them in their house. My friends will never attend my church, so I might as well join with them in their apostate church where the truth is not preached and where godliness is not demanded." If needs be, it is better to weep and lament in the privacy of your home and pour out your heart before God than to join the wicked in their sins.

We have the option that Micah in his day and that the elect remnant in Judah did not have. We can leave the company of the wicked, especially in the false church, and join with God's people in a different location. There are saints living in isolation who say, "Woe unto me," as Micah did, but in many cases nothing is keeping them where they live. They could and should move to a location where there are true Christians and a true church. Micah could not leave because Judah was the church of his day, corrupt as it was. Secession was not an option for him. Since he could not leave the land of Judah, all he could do was lament:

Rivers of waters run down mine eyes, because they keep not thy law. (Ps. 119:136)

5. Woe is me, that I sojourn in Mesech, that I dwell in the tents of Kedar!
6. My soul hath long dwelt with him that hateth peace.
7. I am for peace: but when I speak, they are for war. (120:5–7)

And the LORD said unto him, Go through the midst of the city, through the midst of Jerusalem, and set a mark upon the foreheads of the men that sigh and that cry for all the abominations that be done in the midst thereof. (Ezek. 9:4)

Where secession from the false church and joining a true church is not possible (but do not quickly rule it out: if you were hungry, you would move to where you could eat), such a Christian must pray that God would raise up a source of fellowship in the truth.

MICAH'S DEVOTION

In Micah's sorrow, he turns (and thus encourages the elect remnant and us to turn) to Jehovah: "Therefore I will look unto the LORD" (Mic. 7:7). Looking to Jehovah and waiting on Jehovah are the same activity, the activity of faith.

First, looking to Jehovah means eager expectation. One who looks and waits does so with his eye directed to God, with his heart contemplating God, and with his soul hoping in God. Second, to look means ardent desire: just as a hungry man desires to taste a first ripe fig, so one who looks to and waits on God desires fellowship with God. Third, looking to Jehovah means firm trust.

This is the activity only of a believer who holds for truth what God says in his word and clings to his promises.

Waiting on God is a difficult activity of faith, which is all the more difficult because waiting implies a delay. Jehovah does not answer Micah's prayer immediately, for Jehovah is never in a hurry. His promised salvation is long in preparing, and the longer the delay, the more difficult the wait. The same is true in our individual lives. God promises salvation and glory, but we struggle with sin our whole life long. God calls us to trust him when things are difficult, to wait for the time when his promises will be fulfilled. The same is true for the church: she grows slowly, sometimes painfully slowly. Sometimes it looks like the church will never grow but will only decline. Nevertheless, God's purpose of gathering and defending his elect church continues apace.

We see from verse 7 that devotion to God is a personal matter. Micah calls Jehovah "my God" and "the God of my salvation." That same confession is in the heart and on the lips of every Christian: Jehovah is my God and the God of my children. Jehovah has mercy on me. Jehovah sent his Son to die for my sins and to purchase for me eternal life. "My God," says Micah, "will hear me. Today there is lamentation and deep disappointment, but God will hear my cry, the cry of his elect people who cry day and night to him. He will deliver us."

That is our hope, when the church world has become as cruel to us as a thorn hedge, when good men have perished from the earth. God is with us.

Do not lose heart or despair; Micah did not despair. Do not become impatient or angry. Do not try to take things into your own hands. God's ways are better, for God is wise and good, and the church is in good hands. Cherish and cultivate good fellowship with God's people.

Chapter 16

Penitent Zion's Song of Triumph

8. Rejoice not against me, O mine enemy: when I fall, I shall arise; when I sit in darkness, the Lord shall be a light unto me.

9. I will bear the indignation of the Lord, because I have sinned against him, until he plead my cause, and execute judgment for me: he will bring me forth to the light, and I shall behold his righteousness.

10. Then she that is mine enemy shall see it, and shame shall cover her which said unto me, Where is the Lord thy God? mine eyes shall behold her: now shall she be trodden down as the mire of the streets.

11. In the day that thy walls are to be built, in that day shall the decree be far removed.

12. In that day also he shall come even to thee from Assyria, and from the fortified cities, and from the fortress even to the river, and from sea to sea, and from mountain to mountain.

13. Notwithstanding the land shall be desolate because of them that dwell therein, for the fruit of their doings.

14. Feed thy people with thy rod, the flock of thine heritage, which dwell solitarily in the wood, in the midst of Carmel: let them feed in Bashan and Gilead, as in the days of old.

15. According to the days of thy coming out of the land of Egypt will I shew unto him marvellous things.

16. The nations shall see and be confounded at all their might: they shall lay their hand upon their mouth, their ears shall be deaf.

17. They shall lick the dust like a serpent, they shall move out of their holes like worms of the earth: they shall be afraid of the Lord our God, and shall fear because of thee. (Micah 7:8–17)

In chapter 7, Micah speaks on behalf of the penitent, elect remnant. We saw in the last chapter that the godly in Judah were few and far between. Micah expresses their desire for fellowship and their deep disappointment at not finding it. This leads the godly to confess their confidence in Jehovah (v. 7).

The rest of the chapter deals with Zion's present situation as she looks to the future. Zion is personified as a woman, the daughter of Zion. The rest of the chapter is Daughter Zion's song. The song of Daughter Zion can be divided into different parts with different speakers.

The main speakers in the song are as follows. In verses 8–10, Zion addresses her enemy, also personified as a woman. In verses 11–13, Jehovah addresses Zion with promises. In verse 14, Zion addresses Jehovah with a prayer. In verse 15, Jehovah answers Zion with more promises. In verses 16–20, Zion addresses Jehovah with praise. The song, the chapter, and the book end with a climactic confession of Jehovah's mercy, which we will consider in our final chapter.

CONFESSING HER SINS

At the beginning of the song (v. 8), Zion is in, or is anticipating being in, darkness. The imagery of darkness refers especially to the Babylonian captivity. Perhaps we might think of a dark, gloomy dungeon, a miserable place. Darkness is a fitting word to describe affliction of all kinds in scripture. Darkness is a symbol of death, oppression, or grief. Zion imagines sitting in darkness, for the verb *sitting* indicates a lengthy period of time. Later Jeremiah will prophesy that the Babylonian captivity will be seventy years. The darkness of Zion's captivity will be to see her land desolate (v. 13), to be taken away from the land of Jehovah, and to have no fellowship with him in his temple. This darkness is caused by a fall: "Rejoice not against me, O mine enemy: when I fall" (v. 8). That fall was a fall into apostasy, a departure from the ways of God.

We experience darkness as well: many trials in our lives and especially our sins are for us darkness. Often we find ourselves sitting in darkness for a prolonged period. Perhaps God places us on a bed of sickness so that we feel acutely the infirmities of our flesh. Perhaps God takes from us our livelihood so that for a time we are unemployed and find it difficult to feed our families. Perhaps God brings us through the valley of the shadow of death when we face the death of a loved one or when our own death stares us in the face. Perhaps God brings marital problems, ecclesiastical trials, or even persecution. All of these are forms of darkness by which we are afflicted in this life.

Moreover, Judah is not alone in the darkness, for she has an unwelcome companion. As she languishes in darkness, an enemy, personified as a woman, taunts her. This enemy is Assyria, later Babylon, and ultimately the kingdom of darkness with Satan at its head. When Zion falls into darkness, seduced by the devil, the enemy rejoices against her and addresses her with scornful words of reproach: "Where is the LORD thy God?" (v. 10).

Zion—the elect, believing, penitent remnant with Micah as her spokesman—understands the cause for her sitting in darkness: it is because of her sin. In verse 9, she confesses, "Because I have sinned against him." Zion does not protest her innocence; she does not say that Jehovah has been unfair or unjust in chastising her. Zion remembers her sins, and now she is sorry: she sees that she has brought misery upon herself, and she is willing to sit in darkness until Jehovah is pleased to deliver her. In verse 13, Jehovah reminds Zion, "Notwithstanding the land shall be desolate because of them that dwell therein, for the fruit of their doings."

This must be our confession also when our Father chastises us. To be under the chastisement of God is the experience of darkness. The devil and the world will rejoice when we fall, but we must begin here: "because I have sinned against him." There might not be a particular sin to which we can point, but we know always that we are sinners and therefore it is necessary for us patiently to wait under God's hand.

This is the only way in which we can be content in our trials. When we begin with the truth that God is just, and that he does not treat us as severely as our sins deserve, then our hearts rise to his mercy. The chastisement of Zion in Babylon (placing her in darkness) was necessary for her salvation: "I will bear the indignation of the LORD, because I have sinned against him, until he plead my cause, and execute judgment for me" (v. 9).

We will only be willing cheerfully and patiently to bear the indignation of God if we consider two truths. First, the chastisement that God sends is necessary for our salvation. It is not always easy to see how this can be the case. Doubtless, many in Zion could not see how the Babylonian captivity could serve their salvation. Perhaps there are trials in your life, and you feel as if you are in the dark, and you cannot see the source of the light. That is where you need to exercise faith and say, "I will bear the indignation of the LORD," "He will bring me forth to the light," and "I shall behold his righteousness" (v. 9).

Second, the chastisement that God sends is temporary. Zion does not anticipate being under God's chastening hand forever. She expects that the darkness will eventually come to an end. "Our light affliction, which is but for a moment, worketh for us a far more exceeding and eternal weight of glory" (2 Cor. 4:17). Only with that hope can we possibly remain content under chastisement.

Of course, this can only be true because of another who bore the indignation of God. The indignation of the Lord is the Lord's wrath. There are two types of wrath mentioned in scripture: one is a killing wrath, a wrath that destroys, and the other is a chastening wrath, a wrath that is the expression of God's anger and displeasure. The believer is never the object of God's killing, destroying wrath, but he can be and sometimes is the object of God's fatherly displeasure: "O LORD, rebuke me not in thine anger, neither chasten me in thy hot displeasure" (Ps. 6:1). "Therefore is wrath upon thee from before the LORD" (2 Chron. 19:2).

The reason that the believer cannot be the object of God's eternal wrath in hell, his killing, destroying wrath, is that Christ has borne that in our place. Jesus said, "I will bear the indignation of the LORD" (Mic. 7:9). Impute to me, O God, the sins of all my people, and I will bear their punishment.

EXPRESSING HER HOPE

In the midst of darkness Zion expresses her hope: a certain, future, promised good. Jehovah promises restoration, and Zion lays hold of that promise. Zion's captivity in the darkness shall come to an end. She shall not rot in captivity forever, forgotten by her God and taunted by her enemies. That is why she warns her enemy in verse 8 that her enemy's joy is premature. Darkness and weeping may last for a time, but salvation is coming.

Zion expresses this in terms of light: "The LORD shall be a light unto me" (v. 8); "He will bring me forth to the light" (v. 9). Light is the opposite of darkness: in scripture it is a symbol of life, joy, freedom, salvation, and glory. How fitting that the same hand that places Zion in darkness as a chastisement delivers Zion when the time is right.

We make a similar confession to our enemies when we are under God's hand: "Do not mock me. Do not gloat over me. You may have won the battle, but my God will win the war, and God will use this trial for my good." We must be able to confess that even in the teeth of the devil: "Rejoice not against me, O mine enemy" (v. 8). "I have fallen into sin; you have seduced me, but my God will save me."

The restoration comes with the return from the Babylonian captivity and the rebuilding of Zion. Remember Jehovah's threat in chapter 3:12 that Zion will become heaps, but remember too Jehovah's promise in chapter 4:1 that Zion will be exalted. Chapter 7:11 is the key verse: "In the day that thy walls are to be built."

The word for walls in this passage usually refers to the walls of a vineyard. God broke down the walls in his anger against Zion, but a day is coming when Zion's walls shall be rebuilt. Nevertheless, as is often the case with the prophets, the restoration is greater than the original. In fact, God breaks down the original wall to make way for a better. Micah is not content to prophesy that Zion will be rebuilt, but that Zion will be expanded, increased, and magnified (remember chapter 4:1).

The phrase in verse 11 is somewhat difficult to understand: "In that day shall the decree be far removed." The word translated "decree" has various meanings. It means something prescribed (a prescribed task, a prescribed portion, a prescribed law, or a prescribed limit), and here it most likely means a boundary. The idea is that Jehovah will extend Zion's borders so that her borders are far away. By these words, Jehovah promises to gather the scattered seed of Abraham out of every nation. In other words, verses 11–12 constitute a promise of the gathering of the Gentiles into the New Testament church, which prophecy is being fulfilled throughout the New Testament age.

All of this the daughter of Zion describes in terms of righteousness, judgment, and Jehovah's pleading of her cause (v. 9). Jehovah's righteousness in this passage is his faithfulness to his covenant. The reason God will not and cannot abandon his people is his promise. God has bound himself in love to his people, and he would deny himself if he did not save them. Jehovah wants us to know that so that we can have full confidence in him. That is why the people of God cannot be damned: God has made promises, sworn oaths, and confirmed his word by miracles.

Often we appeal to God's mercy, and we should, but we can equally appeal to his righteousness. That is why Zion answers her enemy, "Rejoice not against me…until he plead my cause" (vv. 8–9). In chapter 6:2, Jehovah had a controversy with his people and he pleads with his people, but in chapter 7:9, Jehovah would plead Zion's cause against her enemies. "Until he…execute judgment for me" (v. 9). Judgment is that which is right, and here it means vindication. Jehovah will vindicate Zion's cause. The same thing is true of us. John writes, "If we confess our sins, he is faithful and just to forgive us our sins, and to cleanse us from all unrighteousness" (1 John 1:9). Quite simply, Jehovah will save everyone whom he loves, whom he has elected, for whom Christ died, and whom the Spirit has regenerated and sanctified. He will never abandon his work.

Jehovah's vindication of Zion includes the destruction of Zion's enemies. Micah uses graphic figures to describe this.

First, in verse 10, Micah promises that the taunting enemy will be ashamed, and that Zion will see the humiliation of her enemies. To be trampled like mud in the streets is to suffer the ultimate humiliation, for Jehovah will not forget those who mistreated his children. Historically, this happened when God destroyed first Assyria, then Babylon, and then every other nation that persecuted his people. This will happen throughout history as God relegates wicked empires to the dustbin of history, and when God finally destroys antichrist and the devil himself.

Second, in verses 16–17, Micah likens the nations who persecute Zion to vile, creeping things and serpents of the earth. They will be thoroughly defeated so that they must lick dust as the serpent. They shall be terrified as they crawl out of their holes to face Jehovah God.

> 10. That at the name of Jesus every knee should bow, of things in heaven, and things in earth, and things under the earth;
> 11. And that every tongue should confess that Jesus Christ is Lord, to the glory of God the Father. (Phil. 2:10–11)

> For he must reign, till he hath put all enemies under his feet. (1 Cor. 15:25)

Do not fret about your enemies, for God will deal with them in his time.

UTTERING HER PLEA

Promises of mercy should drive us to prayer, and this is exactly Zion's response in Micah 7:14. Zion appeals to Jehovah, her faithful shepherd. The idea that Jehovah is Zion's shepherd is found throughout scripture. The verb *feed* in verse 14 means "to shepherd." The rod is the shepherd's rod, a symbol of the shepherd's power and authority, both to lead the sheep and to protect them from their enemies. Zion's prayer is an expression of her utter helplessness: as sheep cannot feed themselves, cannot guide themselves, and cannot protect themselves, so Zion cannot deliver herself. The Christian utters the same prayer: "O Father, I am but a weak, confused, frightened sheep. Life is overwhelming for me. I cannot help myself. All my salvation is of thee."

Zion calls herself Jehovah's "people" and "the flock of [Jehovah's] heritage" (v. 14). This means that Jehovah has chosen Zion (Israel, Judah, and therefore the church) as his own beloved people. He has set his love upon them. They are also a purchased possession: Jesus Christ has purchased them for Jehovah by his own blood on the cross of Calvary. Surely, Jehovah will hear the plaintive cry of his beleaguered, afflicted people. Surely, he will not abandon his heritage. What an incentive we have here to bring our petitions to our Father in heaven through Jesus Christ our savior!

Zion asks that she might dwell safely in Carmel, Bashan, and Gilead as in the days of old (v. 14). Zion looks back to the "good old days" when as a flock of sheep Judah dwelled in the choice pasturelands. Zion longs to graze safely and in abundance under her shepherd's watchful eye. She knows that she has forfeited such a privilege, but she knows equally that Jehovah has promised always to feed her. Therefore, she makes bold to ask God for what he has promised. Our Father is always pleased when we pray to him, laying hold of the promises of his word.

To make this vivid to his Old Testament audience, although less clear to us, the New Testament people of God, Micah identifies three regions of the promised land. The first region is

Carmel, which means "plantation" or "garden land," which is why some Bible versions translate it as "fruitful field," "garden," or "pasture land." One of the best-known inhabitants of Carmel was that old fool Nabal, whose wife, Abigail, David married in 1 Samuel 25.

The second and third regions are Bashan and Gilead. *Bashan* means "smooth," and it was a land on the east of the Jordan River that was rich in grazing for cattle and sheep. Gilead was also on the east of Jordan and was a hill country prized for its grazing. Reuben and Gad were so impressed by Gilead in Numbers 32 that they immediately desired it.

These three regions, then, were not only in the promised land, but were ideal for sheep. Thus it was very natural that Micah would mention these. The desire of Zion, as expressed in this prayer, is to live away from her enemies in peace and safety with Jehovah her covenantal God watching over her and shepherding her.

Jehovah answers his people's prayer with another beautiful promise. His response is basically the promise of a second exodus, but a greater one.

It is interesting that when Jehovah desires to explain redemption and salvation to his people in the Old Testament, he frequently refers back to the exodus: "According to the days of thy coming out of the land of Egypt" (Mic. 7:15). Israel had been in Egypt for some four hundred years, suffering under cruel bondage. While she suffered, she prayed. Jehovah heard her prayers, and he raised up Moses, Aaron, and Miriam to lead his people out of the house of bondage. He worked great wonders in the land of the Egyptians. There are no greater miracles in the whole of the Old Testament than the miracles that God performed by the hand of Moses.

Now Micah promises that Jehovah will again show Zion "marvellous things," the Old Testament term for miracles (v. 15).

The marvelous things were, first, that Jehovah stirred up the heart of the Persian King Cyrus to permit the Israelites to return to the land of Israel, and second, that Jehovah caused the people who returned to rebuild the temple.

But those things, as marvelous as they were, were nothing like the wonders of Egypt. There were no ten plagues of Babylon and no opening of the Red Sea, and the return from Babylon was profoundly disappointing. The marvelous things are the coming of Jesus Christ and the salvation wrought by him. That is the most marvelous, miraculous work of God. We know that is Micah's meaning because of the context. Micah is promising here the restoration of Zion, which includes the gathering of the Gentiles. The exodus out of Egypt was but a dim picture of what Christ did by his death and resurrection; and the return from Babylon was, if anything, a dimmer picture still.

The New Testament in several places, especially 1 Corinthians 10, teaches us that the exodus was designed to instruct us about our salvation in Jesus Christ and our deliverance from the tyranny of the devil and the guilt of our sins. God is showing us in the New Testament age greater miracles than Moses ever wrought or the people of Israel ever saw. What a miracle is the incarnation of the Son of God; what a miracle is the atonement; what a wonder is the resurrection; what a marvelous thing is the ascension; and what a miracle is the outpouring of the Holy Spirit! What a miracle is the salvation of the Gentiles in the New Testament; what a miracle is the destruction of the devil and all his hosts; and what a wonder will be the new heavens and new earth!

Let us lay hold in hope upon these things, although for a time we might have to dwell in the darkness.

Chapter 17

Jehovah:
The Incomparable,
Sin-Pardoning God

18. Who is a God like unto thee, that pardoneth iniquity, and passeth by the transgression of the remnant of his heritage? he retaineth not his anger for ever, because he delighteth in mercy.

19. He will turn again, he will have compassion upon us; he will subdue our iniquities; and thou wilt cast all their sins into the depths of the sea.

20. Thou wilt perform the truth to Jacob, and the mercy to Abraham, which thou hast sworn unto our fathers from the days of old. (Micah 7:18–20)

At the end of Micah the prophet is overwhelmed, and he finishes with a doxology. Micah's doxology echoes two things. First, Micah's name means, "Who is like Jehovah," and it is fitting that Micah ends with, "Who is a God like unto thee?" Second, Micah echoes the song of Moses: "Who is like unto thee, O LORD, among the gods? who is like thee, glorious in holiness, fearful in praises, doing wonders?" (Ex. 15:11). That is why I have entitled this book *Micah: Proclaiming the Incomparable God*, because Jehovah is incomparable in his holiness, power, greatness, judgments, faithfulness, and especially in his mercy.

Micah's doxology is his response to the wonderful promises of salvation in the previous verses. In chapter 7:11, Jehovah promises, despite all of Judah's unfaithfulness and sin, not only to restore Judah, but to expand her borders. In verse 15, Jehovah promises to do wonders that are like (and even greater than) the wonders that Israel saw in the exodus from Egypt.

It is fitting for us to end this book on this doxological note. We need often to be reminded of this great truth of the forgiveness of our sins. There is a danger that we will take our sin-pardoning God for granted. That is a temptation to which many Christians and churches have succumbed, because they no longer mention the forgiveness of sins. To them, forgiveness of sins is old news. Their attitude is, "What has God done for me lately?" We need to savor the text: "Who is a God like unto thee?" (v. 18). Where among the gods of the heathen will we find a god like Jehovah? Which god worshiped by modern man is able to bless as Jehovah can and does? What ought to be our response to this great blessing?

WHAT JEHOVAH DOES

To understand the wonder of forgiveness, we must first understand the horror of sin. The Bible has a very rich and varied vocabulary of sin. Verse 19 uses the word *sins*: "Thou wilt cast all their sins into the depths of the sea." The word *sin* means a missing of the mark. We often think of a person with poor marksmanship. Perhaps a man tries to hit a target, but he misses because he is not good at shooting. With some training and practice he might improve his aim. But that is not what the Bible means by sin: sin in the Bible is a deliberate aiming, shooting at, and hitting another target. The sinner deliberately shoots in the wrong direction. God has set up a target for us at which we must aim our lives, which is his glory. The commandments he gives are a guide by which we might aim at his glory, but we in our sinful pride refuse to aim at his glory, aiming instead at our glory and our pleasure.

Connected to the word *sin* is the word *iniquity*, found in both the singular and plural form in the text: "that pardoneth iniquity" (v. 18) and "he will subdue our iniquities" (v. 19). The word *iniquity* means something twisted or perverted. God is just and righteous, and he has given us a law that is the standard according to which we must walk, but we are twisted and perverse. One guilty of iniquity refuses to conform himself to the righteous standards of God, and he leads a deliberately twisted life. We often think of sexual deviants as perverts, but all sin is iniquity or perversion: lying, stealing, backbiting, covetousness, pride, envy—all of these are iniquities. Iniquity also carries with it the idea of guilt. One who has perverted his way on the earth and has twisted even the good things of this world in the service of sin, deserves to be punished. The sinner, therefore, is one who in his twisted perversion refuses to aim his life at the glory of God but aims it at himself.

This brings us to the third term Micah uses, *transgression*. The word *transgression* is used in verse 18: who "passeth by the transgression of the remnant of his heritage." The word, which means "rebellion," presupposes a relationship of creator-creature or lord-servant. Jehovah is the sovereign lord, while humans are creatures called to be his servants. Transgression is the deliberate and hateful rising up in rebellion of the creature man against Jehovah God. Not only is that wicked, it is also foolish, for who can stand before Jehovah God and hope successfully to rebel against him? Transgression, like sin and iniquity, is deliberate or willful: we willfully trample God's law underfoot in order to serve ourselves and our own pleasures.

We can add to those three words the truth that we are sinners by nature. We are depraved in our hearts and corrupted in our wills, and our whole nature is defiled by sin. That is true of the most moral as well as of the most immoral person.

This doctrine of sin must be preached, explained, believed, and confessed before we can understand and appreciate the wonder that Jehovah forgives. Unless we believe that we too are sinful, depraved, corrupt, rebellious sinners, forgiveness will not mean a lot to us. It is exactly because sin is not preached today that people no longer echo the words of Micah 7:18: "Who is a God like unto thee, that pardoneth iniquity?" Instead we hear, "Who is a God like you who makes me feel good, who lets me live as I please, who gives me nice things, or who helps me change the world?"

Micah describes five great activities that Jehovah alone performs when he forgives, and Micah praises God for these five great activities. First, Jehovah pardons: "that pardoneth iniquity" (v. 18). The Hebrew word translated "pardon" means "to carry, to carry away, and to lift." The idea is of a burden, a burden so heavy that it crushes a person under it. That burden is guilt or iniquity. A guilty man stands before the judge. The guilt of his crimes weighs heavy upon him. He knows that he deserves to be punished. The pardoning judge declares, "I have pardoned you for your crime. I have carried away your guilt. You will not have to bear the punishment." Imagine the relief! What a weight has been removed from his mind and conscience. Micah does not explain how Jehovah does this, but he simply rejoices in the truth of it. Let it sink into your soul: Jehovah pardons iniquity.

Second, connected to that is verse 18: "and passeth by the transgression." To pass by means to walk past something without paying attention to it or deliberately to disregard it. In Luke

10:31–32, the priest and the Levite passed by on the other side and did not pay attention to the suffering of a fellow Jew. Micah uses the verb in a good sense in which Jehovah overlooks, or does not regard, or does not observe, or turns his eyes away from, transgression. Transgression occurs, a rebellion takes place, and sinners rise up in revolt against God, but Jehovah passes by without punishing it. That is forgiveness. Micah does not explain how Jehovah does this, but he simply rejoices in the truth of it. Let it sink into your soul: Jehovah passes by transgression.

Third, Jehovah does not retain his anger: "He retaineth not his anger for ever" (v. 18). To retain is to hold on to something tightly so as not to let it go. The Hebrew verb means "to strengthen." Jehovah does not strengthen himself in anger. Jehovah has every right to be angry and to express his anger in punishing us. Instead, Jehovah lets go of his anger and turns his anger away. Micah does not explain how Jehovah does this; he simply rejoices in the truth of it. Let it sink into your soul: Jehovah does not retain his anger.

Fourth, Jehovah subdues iniquity: "He will subdue our iniquities" (v. 19). To subdue means to conquer, to overpower, or to bring into subjection. Our sins have subjection over us, they rule us, and they enslave us. But Jehovah subdues our sins so we have power over them and are free to serve him. This shows us that salvation includes sanctification. We are not forgiven so that we can go on sinning, but we are forgiven so that we serve God.

Fifth, and finally, Micah uses a beautiful figurative expression, for so great is Jehovah's destruction of our sins that he casts them into the sea. Take a ship into the middle of the Atlantic Ocean where the average depth is over three kilometers or two miles. Drop an object into the ocean, and you will never see it again, for the billows of the ocean have swallowed it. Jehovah does that with our sins: all our sins are thrown into the sea. They will never come back to haunt us, and God will never hold them against us. This is a greater wonder than the drowning of Pharaoh and his host: "I will sing unto the LORD, for he hath triumphed gloriously: the horse and his rider hath he thrown into the sea" (Ex. 15:1). We can sing, "I will sing unto the LORD, for he hath triumphed gloriously: all our sins hath he thrown into the sea."

WHY JEHOVAH DOES THIS

Jehovah forgives, says Micah, "because he delighteth in mercy" (v. 18). *Mercy* is a very important word in the Bible, but many Christians have an inadequate understanding of its meaning. The most common misunderstanding of mercy is to equate mercy with God not giving someone what he deserves. A judge is merciful when he spares a criminal who deserves prison and gives him either no punishment, a lesser punishment, or a delayed punishment. Therefore, if God does not punish a sinner or if he does not yet punish a sinner and in the meantime gives him more time to repent and to enjoy the good things of creation, we are told that that he is merciful.

But that is not the biblical definition of mercy: mercy is fundamentally something else. Mercy is tender affection and pity or compassion upon those who are miserable. When you see mercy in the Bible, always think of two things: compassion and misery. In the Bible the objects of God's mercy are miserable; for example, it is the poor, the blind, the leprous who cry out for mercy and receive it. The self-righteous, the proud, and those who have no sense of their true misery (which is sin) do not receive mercy, unless God mercifully changes their hearts. Mercy is always the compassionate response of someone to misery.

Mercy therefore is the compassionate attitude of God's heart toward a miserable person. That comes out clearly in verse 19:

"He will turn again; he will have compassion upon us." The Hebrew verb *to have compassion* comes from the word for *bowels*. Hebrew thought located the emotions in the intestinal organs. "Is Ephraim my dear son? is he a pleasant child? for since I spake against him, I do earnestly remember him still: therefore my bowels are troubled for him; I will surely have mercy upon him, saith the LORD" (Jer. 31:20).

Jehovah's mercy never remains a mere attitude of pity or compassion for the miserable. Jehovah's mercy is active: he seeks out and finds the miserable, and he lifts them out of their misery in order to make them blessed.

In this mercy Jehovah delights: "because he delighteth in mercy" (Mic. 7:18). Jehovah takes pleasure in his own mercy. He admires his own mercy, for it is perfect, holy, righteous mercy. It gives him great pleasure to show mercy. Jehovah never reluctantly or begrudgingly shows mercy. We must not think that Jehovah is poor in mercy, for he is rich in mercy. Jehovah is abundant in mercy, and his mercy is from everlasting to everlasting. If Jehovah's mercy could dry up, come to an end, or, worse, change into wrath, how poor would his mercy be! It is because of Jehovah's mercy that a miserable people such as Judah could rejoice in it, even after so many prophecies of terrible judgment. It is because of Jehovah's eternal, unfailing, and faithful mercy that we, the New Testament church of Jesus Christ, can have such hope and confidence.

Do you know the mercy of Jehovah? Do you experience in your heart and life the sweetness of the forgiveness of sins that Jehovah delights to show? Jehovah delights in mercy because it is his own mercy, and it gives him great pleasure to glorify himself by lifting miserable sinners out of misery and causing them to taste and know his own mercy and goodness.

Before Jehovah shows mercy to any creature, Jehovah *is* mercy. Mercy is an attribute of God, something he is within himself and to himself. God's mercy in himself is his delighting in himself as the sum total of all perfection and knowing himself as most blessed forever. Moreover, Jehovah determined within himself not to keep his blessedness to himself, not to hide his mercy within his own being, but to display it, to share it, to give it. He delights to do this because in this way he glorifies himself, and he delights to glorify himself and have us praise him for his mercy.

The second main reason for Jehovah's forgiving sinners is his faithfulness or truth. Verse 20 ends that way: "Thou wilt perform the truth." Truth is something firm and solid, and therefore something upon which one might lean or support oneself. Jehovah himself is the truth. The name *Jehovah* emphasizes that this God is truth: he is the unchanging, unchangeable, utterly faithful God of the covenant who keeps his promises. Micah can be so confident of the forgiveness of sins because Jehovah has promised to forgive the sins of his people. Jehovah promised salvation, and Jehovah's promise cannot fail.

On those two solid pillars is built the foundation of our salvation: God is faithful and God is merciful. Therefore, it is impossible for the church to perish. God swore that to Abraham, to Jacob, and to all the fathers from the days of old.

It is striking that the prophets are always harkening back to the days of old, to the earlier promises of God, because they know that God will fulfill his word. Abraham lived over one thousand years before Micah prophesied, but Micah *still* described salvation in terms of the promise to Abraham, Isaac, and Jacob. It was according to that promise that Jesus Christ came, in whom we have the forgiveness of sins. This faithfulness or truth is also an important consideration in this question: whose sins does Jehovah forgive, or to whom does Jehovah delight to show mercy?

The answer is given clearly in verse 18: "the remnant of his heritage." Jehovah does not forgive the sins of everyone. Jehovah is not merciful to everyone. Jehovah does not pass by the transgression of everyone. Jehovah does not cast everyone's sins into the depths of the sea. Instead, Jehovah forgives a remnant. The majority of the people of the northern and southern kingdoms of Israel and Judah he does not forgive. Jehovah forgives the true people of God, the elect kernel within the nation, the spiritual Israel. They are the remnant of Jehovah's heritage. That means that Jehovah saves us, for when Jehovah made promises to Abraham, he made promises to Christ, and when he made promises to Christ, he made promises to us (Gal. 3:16, 29).

That is because all those who believe in Jesus Christ, whether Jew or Gentile, are the children of Abraham and heirs according to the promise. God promised to Abraham, "In thee shall all families of the earth be blessed" (Gen. 12:3). That was a promise to send a descendant of Abraham (the Bible calls him the "seed" of Abraham) through whom salvation, mercy, and forgiveness of sins would come, not only to the elect, believing, physical descendants of Abraham, but to believers from all nations under heaven. Thank God that one does not have to be a physical descendant of Abraham in order to receive the mercy of God!

HIS INCOMPARABLENESS IN DOING THIS

The fulfillment of God's promise of mercy is found in Jesus Christ. It is only in Jesus Christ that two things can be true—first, Jehovah forgives sins; and second, Jehovah satisfies his own justice. There seems to be a problem. How can Jehovah forgive sins and remain just? How can Jehovah pardon (or carry away) sin? How can Jehovah pass by transgression? How can Jehovah let go of his anger? How can Jehovah subdue iniquity? And how can Jehovah cast sins into the depths of the sea?

If an earthly judge disregarded the crimes of guilty people, he would be unjust. How, then, can the perfect judge forgive sinners such as we are? Jehovah cannot simply forgive sins by an act of his sovereign power and will. His justice must be satisfied. In Exodus 34:7, Jehovah reveals to Moses this about himself, as part of his name: "Keeping mercy for thousands, forgiving iniquity and transgression and sin, and that will by no means clear the guilty." Jehovah will not clear the guilty—how, then, does he forgive sin?

The answer is found in Jesus Christ. Throughout the Old Testament, God revealed that his justice could only be satisfied by sacrifices. But the people understood that the blood of animals could never take away sins. The sacrifices of the Old Testament were designed to prepare for and teach about a better sacrifice. The true sacrifice is the sacrifice of the Son of God on the cross. Therefore, the way in which Jehovah delights to show mercy and pardon sins is in Christ Jesus.

Jehovah pardons iniquity, which means that he lifts the burden of sin and he places that burden of sin on Christ, who carries it for us. Jesus carried that burden of guilt to the cross, where he suffered and died on account of it, thus removing the burden forever. When the Judge says, "Not guilty. You will not carry the burden of guilt," that is because Jesus Christ was punished in our place for us.

Jehovah passes by transgression, which means that he overlooks it and will not regard it. The righteous God cannot simply ignore rebellion; therefore, that rebellion was not disregarded. Instead, Jehovah imputed the guilt of that rebellion to Jesus Christ and punished him for it. He who deserved to be spared was not spared, so that we who do not deserve to be spared are spared (Rom. 8:32).

Jehovah does not retain his anger forever. The reason Jehovah does not hold on tightly to his wrath is that he unleashed his anger upon Jesus Christ. Jehovah turned in all his fury to his Son and made his Son the object of his wrath on the cross.

Jehovah subdues our iniquities because Christ crushed the power of our iniquity on the cross. By dying on the cross, Christ destroyed the power of sin, the devil, death, the world, and hell. By rising from the dead, he brings new life to those whom the Father has given him.

Jehovah casts our sins into the depths of the sea because he caused his Son to descend into the depths of his wrath, as he plunged his own Son under the billows of his wrath. Psalm 69:1–2 describes the anguish of the Son of God on the cross: "Save me, O God; for the waters are come in unto my soul. I sink in deep mire, where there is no standing: I am come into deep waters, where the floods overflow me."

If our sins are plunged into the depths of the sea, Jesus himself was plunged into the wrath of God, under God's curse, there to pay the price of our rebellion. The mercy of God is not seen in God ignoring sin. Rather, it is seen in God sending his Son to take the place of miserable, guilty, hell-deserving sinners.

Surely, the only fitting response is Micah's: "Who is a God like unto thee?" Are there any other gods who do this, and who do it in the way that Jehovah does? Many in Judah had forsaken Jehovah for the gods of the heathen. When King Ahaz was in the Valley of Hinnom offering his son to the god Molech (2 Chronicles 28), he had forsaken Jehovah the incomparable, sin-pardoning God. When the prophets of Baal in Elijah's day were cutting themselves with knives and lancets (1 Kings 18), they had forsaken Jehovah the incomparable, sin-pardoning God.

Today it is exactly the same: will the modern gods of mankind compare to Jehovah, the incomparable, sin-pardoning God? The god of pleasure will take you, abuse you, and spit you out.

Observe the drunkard in the gutter, the drug addict in a dark alley or in a prison cell, or the sexually promiscuous in the hospital or in the morgue: where is the mercy in those gods? Cruel and heartless as the devil are those gods. What solace, comfort, or mercy is found in those gods? None!

Micah's last words are a doxology and a call to repentance. Seek mercy in Jehovah God, and turn from your gods, for Jehovah delights to show mercy to penitent sinners. "Let the wicked forsake his way, and the unrighteous man his thoughts: and let him return unto the LORD, and he will have mercy upon him; and to our God, for he will abundantly pardon" (Isa. 55:7). Are your sins as scarlet? Believe in the Lord Jesus Christ, and the merciful God will make them as white as snow. Are they red like crimson? Believe in the Lord Jesus Christ, and the merciful God will make them as wool (Isa. 1:18). We come to Jesus Christ with the crushing burden of guilt, and the merciful God removes our guilt and gives us peace. We come oppressed by our iniquities, and the merciful God sends our iniquities away. What a message of hope for the elect, believing remnant in Judah! What a message of hope for believers in Christ in every age!

Let us take our leave from Micah the prophet. Let us heed his warnings, and let us embrace his promises. Above all, let us look to Jehovah, the incomparable, sin-pardoning God, through Jesus Christ our Lord. For who is a God like unto him?

ABOUT THE AUTHOR

Martyn McGeown grew up in County Tyrone, Northern Ireland, is a member of the Covenant Protestant Reformed Church in Ballymena, Northern Ireland, graduated from the Theological School of the Protestant Reformed Churches in June 2010, and has been the missionary-pastor of the Limerick Reformed Fellowship in Limerick, Ireland, since July 2010. He is the author of *Called to Watch for Christ's Return* and *Grace and Assurance: The Message of the Canons of Dordt.*

www.ingramcontent.com/pod-product-compliance
Lightning Source LLC
Chambersburg PA
CBHW060753100426
42813CB00004B/796